Teddy Bear Figurines
Price Guide

BY

Jesse Murray

ACKNOWLEDGEMENTS

I would like to thank the following companies and their staff for their invaluable time in producing information and photographs for this book: Anna-Perenna® Porcelain, Inc.; Bialosky Treasury; Boyds Collection LTD; Cast Art Industries; Cavanagh Group International; Crystal World®; Department 56®; Enesco® Corporation; Fort®, Inc.; Franklin Mint; Ganz, Inc.; Great American® Taylor Collectible Corporation; L. L. Knickerbocker Company, Inc.; Nevenschwander Artworks; North American Bear Company, Inc.; Pacific Rim Import, Corporation; Penni Jo's Originals; Raikes Originals; Russ® Berrie and Company, Inc.; Sarah's Attic®, Inc.; Schmid; Steiff USA, L. P.; United Design® Corporation; VickiLane Creative Design; and the Sea Island Business Center.

A special thanks to Hobby House Press for making this book available to the thousands of teddy bear figurine collectors worldwide. Thanks to Mary Beth Ruddell, my editor, for her editorial guidance.

Also a very special thanks to my mother and father for their support and faith in my career goal of becoming a professional artist and published writer.

Front Cover: Left to Right: *Dress-Up,* Cuddl'somes™, Cast Art Industries; *Murray and Sweetie,* Teddy Angels™, United Design® Corporation; *Christopher, "Old Friends Are The Best Friends",* 1992 TOBY® Award Winner, Cherished Teddies®, Enesco®; *The Lesson,* 1995 TOBY® Award Winner, Bearstone™ Collection, Boyds Collection LTD; *Eight Polar Bears,* Coco-Cola® Heritage Collection, Cavanagh Group International; and *Henrietta's Tea Party,* Upstairs, Downstairs Bears™, Department 56®.

Title Page: *Wilson with Love Sonnets:* issued 1993, resin, artist: Gary Lowenthal, Bearstone™ Collection, Boyds Collection LTD.

Back Cover: *Shawnie* with Papoose and *Nathan* with a Bounty of Corn, 1995 TOBY® Award Nomination, Chapelle Noelle™, Enesco®; *Giddy-Up,* Joy Bears™, Fort®, Inc.; *Teddy Rose and Bully Dog,* Steiff USA, L.P.; *Proxy with Jewelry Box,* Michaud Collection, Sarah's Attic®.

Published by  Hobby House Press, Inc.
Grantsville, Maryland 21536

Additional copies of this book may be purchased at $19.95 (plus postage and handling) from
Hobby House Press, Inc.
1 Corporate Drive
Grantsville, Maryland 21536
1-800-554-1447
or from your favorite bookstore or dealer.

ISBN: 0-87588-448-2

TABLE OF CONTENTS

Grenville the Storyteller, the Bearstone™ Collection.

Lost and Lonely, the Cuddl'somes™ Collection.

"Always Cool" Polar Bear, Coca-Cola® Heritage Collection.

Joan, the Chapeau Noelle™ Collection.

TABLE OF CONTENTS

Letter to Santa, the PennyWhistle Lane Collection.

Pilot, the Teddy Town™ Collection.

Reach for the Stars, the Joy Bears™ Collection.

Bruin and Bluebirds, Teddy Angels™ Collection.

INTRODUCTION

This book is designed to introduce the collector to some of the more popular teddy bear figurine collections available on today's market by providing company histories, artist biographies, full color photographs of teddy bear figurines for easy photo identification, a list of club information on several teddy bear collections, and an easy to follow price index.

As teddy bear figurine collecting grows, it becomes more difficult for the producer to create material tracing the history of the collection, and describing minute detail about every item in the collection. This is where this book becomes an invaluable tool for the collector. With the latest information on your favorite teddy bear figurine collection, everything is right at your fingertips, in a handy, easy to read format.

Today, Teddy Bear figurine collections offer an array of different mediums and styles to the collector. The trend of collecting teddy bear figurines is growing with popularity and becoming highly collectible in the collectible market. In researching this book, I have listed several tips for a collector to remember when buying and collecting their favorite teddy bear collection. These tips will help the collector in their many enjoying hours of collecting teddy bear figurines.

TIPS TO REMEMBER WHEN COLLECTING TEDDY BEAR FIGURINES

1) Buy teddy bear figurines for your pleasure and needs; avoid buying for speculative investment purposes, especially over a long term.

2) Read books and subscribe to magazines in the collectible field. Keep up-to date on trends and new collections.

3) Try to purchase all pieces in a specific collection or series.

4) Buy two of the same figurine, if possible. Keep one still packaged in original box for collectible status, and the other to display for enjoyment.

5) Always purchase any limited edition pieces available in a collection.

6) Join collectible clubs offered by teddy bear figurine collections. Clubs can give the collector first hand information on retired pieces, new releases, and the opportunity to purchase pieces only available to club members.

7) Attend all artist signings and events. Signed figurines are a special buying incentive on the secondary market.

8) Purchase retiring figurines before they go to the secondary market.

9) Buy from the secondary market only when searching for retired pieces and closed limited editions to complete your figurine collection.

10) Collect several figurine quotes before purchasing on the secondary market. This will help protect you from paying too much for a certain piece. But remember the value you pay is determined by the desire to add the piece to your collection.

ANNA-PERENNA® PORCELAIN, INC.

ADORABLES™ COLLECTION

Anna-Perenna® Porcelain, an international firm specializing in limited edition art plates made of hard-paste Bavarian porcelain, miniature figurines and limited edition sculptures, was founded in 1977 by Kaus D. Vogt, the former President of Rosenthal, U. S. A. Initial work included translating the art of Thaddeus Krumeich, Count Bernzdotte, Al Hirschfeld and foremost Pat Buckley Moss, into limited edition plates.

Anna-Perenna® Porcelain also produces a unique collection of limited edition porcelain figurines designed by P. Buckley Moss.

In 1989 Anna-Perenna® introduced Adorables™ Collection, a collection of miniatures by Scottish Artist Peter Fagan. These whimsical pieces, inspired by Fagan's plush antique teddy bears, have generated thousands of loyal collectors in the United States and Europe. Each incredibily detailed bear in the Adorables™ Collection tells a specific story which is found with the figurine. The figurines are cast in Kaomingh™* and hand-painted. The collection consists of single teddies and teddies set in environments to match their features and traits.

The Adorables™ Collection was retired in 1994. Today these highly collectible figurines have doubled their issue price on the secondary market.

*Kaomingh™ is a cold-cast material whose name is derived from "kaolin" (porcelain clay) and "ming," the Chinese era in which porcelain-making reached its greatest heights.

*See Enesco® for information about artist Peter Fagan.

1. *Humphrey:* issued 1989, 2-1/2in (6cm), cast in Kaomingh™, retired 1994.

1

2

3

4

5

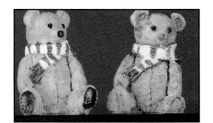

6

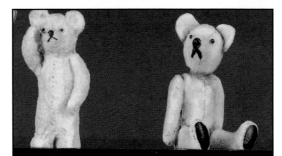

7

8

9

LEFT to RIGHT:

2. ***Theodore:*** issued 1989, 1-1/4in (3.65cm), cast in Kaomingh™, retired 1994; ***Teddy Robinson:*** issued 1989, 1in (3cm), cast in Kaomingh™, retired 1994; ***Johann:*** issued 1989, 1-1/4in (3.65cm), cast in Kaomingh™, retired 1994.

3. ***Peter Bear:*** issued 1989, 2in (5cm), cast in Kaomingh™, retired 1994.

4. ***Gustav Von Bruin:*** issued 1989, 1-3/4in (5cm), cast in Kaomingh™, retired 1994; ***Dickie Bear:*** issued 1989, 1-3/8in (3.9cm), cast in Kaomingh™, retired 1994; ***Robert:*** issued 1989, 1-5/8in (5cm), cast in Kaomingh™, retired 1994.

5. ***Red Scarf; Blue Scarf;*** issued 1989, 1in (3cm), cast in Kaomingh™, retired 1994.

6. ***Jonathan:*** issued 1989, 1-3/8in (3.9cm), cast in Kaomingh™, retired 1994; ***Peregrine:*** issued 1989, 1-1/4in (3.65cm), cast in Kaomingh™, retired 1994.

7. ***Fluffy:*** issued 1989, 1-1/4in (3.65cm), cast in Kaomingh™, retired 1994.

8. ***Chocolate Chip:*** 1-1/4in (3.65cm); ***Ben:*** 1-1/4in (3.65cm); ***Irvine:*** 1-1/2in (4cm). All issued 1991, cast in Kaomingh™, all retired 1994.

9. ***August String Bear,*** issued 1989, 1-5/8in (5cm), cast in Kaomingh™, retired 1994.

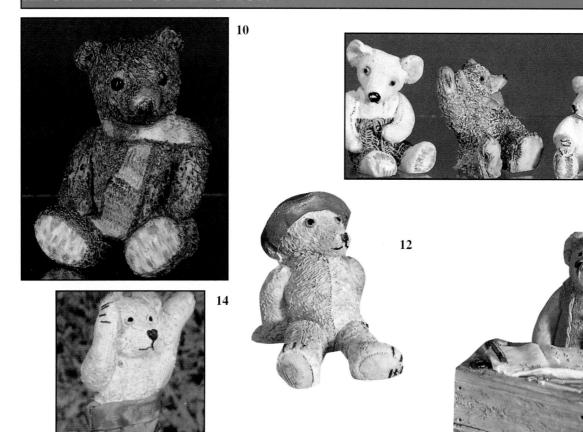

10

11

12

13

14

15

16

10. ***Bruno:*** issued 1989,
    2-1/4in (5.65cm), cast
    in Kaomingh™, retired 1994.
11. ***Mr. Perkins:*** 1-3/4in (5cm); ***Shiner:***
    1-1/2in (4cm); ***Tinker Thomas:***
    1-1/2in (4cm). All issued 1991, cast
    in Kaomingh™, all retired 1994.
12. ***Derek:*** issued 1991, 2in (5cm), cast
    in Kaomingh™, retired 1994.
13. ***Educating Timmy:*** issued 1991,
    4-1/4in (10.65cm), cast in
    Kaomingh™, retired 1994.
14. ***Bernard:*** issued 1990,
    2-3/4in (7cm), cast in Kaomingh™,
    retired 1994.
15. ***Barrow Boy:*** issued 1991,
    4in (10cm), cast in Kaomingh™,
    retired 1994.
16. ***Baron Von Berne:*** issued 1991,
    2-3/4in (7cm), cast in
    Kaomingh™, retired 1994.

BOYDS BEAR COLLECTION LTD.

THE BEARSTONE™ COLLECTION

The Bearstone™ Collection was started in early 1992 by creator Gary Lowenthal. The collection captures a combination of aesthetics and craftmanship. These figurines are sculptural interpretations of the now famous plush bears, hares, tabbies, mooses and other friends of the Boyds Bear Collection LTD.

Each figurine in the Bearstone™ Collection starts with Lowethal's conceptualized sketch. The piece is then sculpted and cold cast in resin. Each piece is hand-painted, individually numbered and comes with a Certificate of Authenticity signed by Gary

Lowenthal. A unique symbol of authenticity is a hidden paw print on each piece.

The detailed figurines range in sizes measuring 4 to 5-1/2 inches high. Each one has its own special theme or mood. As of 1995, The Bearstone™ Collection has over 75 pieces. There are plans for it to grow even larger.

The award-winning Bearstone™ Collection has sparked world-wide interest and is a growing collectible in the secondary market.

33

33. *Miss Bruin and Bailey...the Lesson:* won 1995 Toby® Award, issued 1995, cast in resin, open edition.

34

35

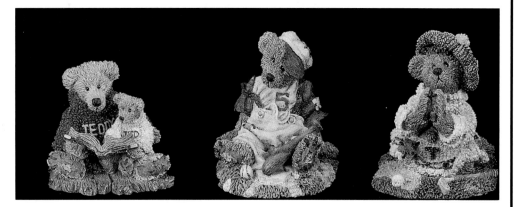

36

37

About the Artist:
GARY M. LOWENTHAL

Gary M. Lowenthal, chief designer, president and head bear of the Boyds Collection LTD, was born in New York City in 1949. Raised on Manhattan Island, he quickly learned to appreciate all that the Big Apple had to offer. He received a B.S. and a M.S. in Biology from Alfred University in upstate New York, and then joined the U. S. Peace Corps. After his tour of the world, he returned to New York where he began a seven year career of purchasing, designing, and merchandising at Bloomingdales. Here he was exposed to the great designers of New York, Paris, London and Tokyo.

Lowenthal took his bold step and moved to Boyds, Maryland, to start The Boyds Collection LTD., in an out-of-the-way antique shop. With his clothing design experience, he decided to start a line of hand-carved wood duck decoys.

Working out of a restored 1800 farmhouse, Gary built his business and began designing miniature ceramic houses (The Gnomes Homes) as well as the duck decoys. In 1987, Gary turned his hand to teddy bears, and, with Gae Sharp (world famous teddy bear designer), began designing a line of collectible teddy bears, hares, tabbies, and pooches. The present plush line encompasses over 300 different styles from 3 inch miniatures to 21 inch giants. Many have received awards and nominees, and each year limited editions are issued.

34. *Bailey Bear with Suitcase*; *Simone De Bearvoire and Her Mom; Neville the Bedtime Bear.* All issued 1993, cast in resin, open edition.
35. *Justina and M. Harrison; Grenville and Beatrice...Best Friends.* All issued 1994, cast in resin, open edition.
36. *Ted and Teddy; Homer on the Plate; Sebastian's Prayer.* All issued 1994, cast in resin, open edition.
37. *Bailey in the Orchard:* issued 1993, cast in resin, open edition.

38

39

40

41

42

43

38. *Victoria...the Lady:* issued 1993; *Bailey's Birthday:* issued 1994; *Bailey and Wixie...to Have and to Hold:* issued 1994; *Sherlock and Watson in Disguise:* issued 1994. All cast in resin, open edition.
39. *Wilson with Love Sonnets; Christian by the Sea.* All issued 1993, cast in resin, open edition.
40. *Bailey and Emily...Forever Friends:* issued 1994, cast in resin, open edition.
41. *Wilson at the Beach:* issued 1994, cast in resin, open edition.
42. *Grenville and Neville...the Sign:* issued 1993; *Wilson the Perfesser:* issued 1994. All cast in resin, open edition.
43. *Clara the Nurse:* issued 1994, cast in resin, open edition.

44

45

46

47

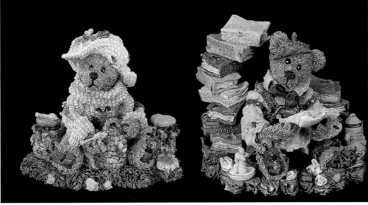

48

44. *Agatha and Shelly...Scaredy Cat:* issued 1994; *Wilson...the Wonderful Wizard of Wuz:* issued 1995; *Emma...the Witchy Bear:* issued 1995. All cast in resin, open edition.

45. *Knute and the Gridiron:* issued 1994; *Hop-along...the Deputy:* issued 1995; *Otis...the Fisherman:* issued 1995. All cast in resin, open edition.

46. *Grenville the Graduate:* issued 1994, cast in resin, open edition.

47. *Grenville and Knute...Football Buddies; Union Jack...Love Letters.* All issued 1995, cast in resin, open edition.

48. *Bailey...the Honey Bear; Otis...Taxtime:* issued 1995, cast in resin, open edition.

49

50

51

52

53

49. *Angelica...the Guardian; Simone and Bailey...Helping Hands;*
    Bailey...the Cheerleader. All issued 1995, cast in resin, open edition.
50. *Grenville the Santabear; Kringle and Bailey with List; Elgin the Elf*
    Bear. All issued 1994, cast in resin, open edition.
51. *Edmund and Bailey Gathering Holly:* issued 1994, cast in resin,
    open edition.
52. *Elliot and the Tree; Elliot and Snowbeary.* All issued 1994, cast in
    resin, open edition.
53. *Grenville the Storyteller:* first limited edition, issued 1995, cast in
    resin, retired December 1995.

54

55

56

57

58

59

60

54. ***The Stage...the School Pageant: Theresa as Mary; Baldwin as the Child; Neville as Joseph.*** All issued 1995, cast in resin, open edition.
55. ***Arthur with Green Scarf:*** issued 1993, retired December 1993; ***Moriarty the Bear in the Cat Suit:*** issued 1993, retired December 1995, ***Grenville with Red Scarf:*** issued 1993, retired December 1995. All cast in resin.
56. ***Bailey at the Beach; Clarence Angel Bear.*** Both issued 1994, cast in resin, retired December 1995.
57. ***Arthur with Red Scarf:*** issued 1993, cast in resin, retired in December 1994.
58. ***Bailey...the Baker:*** nominated for 1995 TOBY® Award, issued 1995, cast in resin, open edition.
59. ***Juliette Angel Bear:*** issued 1994, cast in resin, retired December 1995.
60. ***Father Chrisbear and Son:*** issued 1993, cast in resin, retired December 1993.

CAST ART INDUSTRIES, INC.

Cast Art Industries was founded in December 1990 by Scott Sherman, Fran Colapinto and Gary Barsellotti, three friends with more than fifty years of combined experience in the gift industry. Sherman was formerly a Florida corporate president, who despite his youth, has had substantial experience in administration and marketing. Colapinto, a long time resident of California, has spent most of his career building a national sales force in the gift industry. Barselotti, Italian-born and trained, is an expert in the manufacturing of fine quality figurines.

Just over four years ago, California-based Cast Art Industries took the collectible gift market by storm with the introduction of the now-popular Dreamsicles® collection. Since that time, the company has produced the works of additional talented artists representing a wide range of styles and subjects. The result is an exciting array of collectible figurines certain to please any collector.

Cast Art Industries, Inc., introduced its Cuddl'somes™ Teddy Bear figurine collection in early 1995. The initial response was far greater than anticipated, exceeding even their successful Dreamsicles®. This collection of 52 bears and other adorable animal figurines is based on several original designs of renowned artists Kristin Haynes, Steve Hackett and Gigi Hackett.

Each figurine in the Cuddl'somes™ collection is intricately detailed and hand-painted to perfection. These adorable figurines are then hand numbered and may be registered for collectibility.

Cuddl'somes™ features fanciful characters including teddy bear pirates, cowboys, firemen and sports figures, as well as delightful cows, pigs and more.

This unique collection of precious teddy bears and their adorable animal friends is designed and priced right, making the collection an instant winner.

Cuddl'somes™ figurines were nominated for the 1995 Sixth Annual TOBY® Awards which recognize the outstanding achievement in the design, workmanship and manufacture of Teddy Bears, and were nominated by members of the international Teddy Bear Society. "Cubby," a little baseball player, and sweet little "Dress Up" bear were both nominated in the category of Figurine Bear Manufacturer.

The popularity of this line has led to Cast Art's introduction of Cuddl'somes™ water globes and Christmas ornaments. Cast Art has also signed an exclusive licensing agreement with Confetti, Inc. of Edison, New Jersey to manufacture plush toy versions of several of the Cuddl'somes™ designs.

61. *The Happy Couple:* issued 1995, 4-1/4in (10.65cm), cast in resin, open edition.

About the Artist:
KRISTIN HAYNES

Ten years ago, artist Kristin Haynes turned her talents to sculpture and began creating unique, adorable cherubs which became popular with fans in southern California. Demand grew so great that Kristin could no longer make reproductions in sufficient quantities on her own.

Kristin showed her samples to Cast Art Industries, a quality gift manufacturing company, which quickly saw the potential in the artist's fresh style. Cast Art recognized that to be successful, the line must maintain its unique characteristics; reproductions would be handcrafted using the finest natural materials, hand-painted, and offered as collectibles at an affordable price. The line was named Dreamsicles® and introduced to the public in March 1991. Among the fastest-growing lines in the history of collectibles, Dreamsicles® have consistently been named America's number one seller in monthly surveys of gift retailers. Kristin's newest creation, Cuddl'somes™ are sure to follow with much success.

About the Artists:
STEPHEN & GIGI HACKETT

Collectors in search of rising young stars will want to familiarize themselves with the work of Steve and Gigi Hackett, a talented husband-and-wife team who's figurines were recently introduced by Cast Art Industries, Inc.

Steve apprenticed with the Disney® organization and left to undertake freelance commissions, one-of-a-kind sculptures for the rich and famous, and a soon-to-be-released animated series. Collaborating with his wife Gigi, a unique team approach and sense of humor has resulted in two new collectible series.

Animal Attractions is an assortment of humorous portrayals of favorite four-legged friends, including "flasher" cows, bikini-clad pigs and dancing bears. Story Time Treasures are representations of beloved children's stories, from "The Three Little Pigs" to "The Frog Prince," each depicts a parent animal reading to his youngster.

These delightful works are available as collectible figurines and children's lamps. Like all Cast Art products, the reproductions are painstakingly hand-cast and hand-painted.

Steve and Gigi Hackett represent a fresh new wave of young California artists who's work is beginning to attract nationwide attention.

62

64

63

62. *Cuddl'somes Logo:* issued 1995, 6-1/2in (16cm), cast in resin, open edition.
63. *Big Big Hug:* issued 1995, 3in (8cm), cast in resin, open edition.
64. *Sparky, Fireman Teddy Bear:* issued 1995, 1-3/4in (5cm), cast in resin, open edition.

LEFT to RIGHT: **65**
65. *Winchester:* issued 1995, 4in (10cm), cast in resin, open edition.
     Sidekick: issued 1995, 3-3/4in (10cm), cast in resin, open edition.
     Sundance: issued 1995, 5-1/4in (13.65cm), cast in resin, open edition.
     Howdy (Mini): issued 1995, 2-1/4in (8.65cm), cast in resin, open edition.

LEFT to RIGHT: **66**

66.   ***Tiny Tim (Mini):*** issued 1995, 2in (5cm), cast in resin, open edition.
      Beary Christmas: issued 1995, 3-1/2in (9cm), cast in resin, open edition.
      Rupert: issued 1995, 3-1/2inches (9cm), cast in resin, open edition.
      Snuggles: issued 1995, 2in (5cm), cast in resin, open edition.

OPPOSITE PAGE: LEFT to RIGHT:

67.   ***School Days (Mini):*** issued 1995, 2-1/2in (6cm), cast in resin, open edition.
      Sugar Ray (Mini): issued 1995, 2in (5cm), cast in resin, open edition.
      Touchdown Bear (Mini): issued 1995, 2-1/4in (5.65cm), cast in resin, open edition.
      Rah-Rah (Mini): issued 1995, 2in (5cm), cast in resin, open edition.

68

LEFT to RIGHT:
68. ***Bacon and Eggs:*** issued 1995, 3in (8cm), cast in resin, open edition.
Keystone: issued 1995, 4-1/4in (10.65cm), cast in resin, open edition.
At the Malt Shop: issued 1995, 4-1/2in (11cm), cast in resin, open edition.
We Need Love: issued 1995, 3-3/4 in (10cm), cast in resin, open edition.

69

70

71

69. ***Dress Up:*** issued 1995, 1995 TOBY® Awards nominee,
    5in (13cm), cast in resin, open edition.
70. ***Cubby:*** issued 1995, 1995 TOBY® Awards nominee,
    3-1/2in (9cm), cast in resin, open edition.
71. ***Roosevelt:*** issued 1995, 5in (13cm), cast in resin, open edition.

72

73

74

75

72. *Abbie Lou:* issued 1995, 3in (8cm), cast in resin, open edition.
73. *Two A.M. Feeding:* issued 1995, 3-1/2in (9cm), cast in resin, open edition.
74. *Tea for Two:* issued 1995, 4-1/2in (11cm), cast in resin, open edition.
75. *Ice Dancer:* issued 1995, 3-1/2in (9cm).

76

LEFT to RIGHT:
76. **Scare Bear:** issued 1995, 5in (13cm), cast in resin, open edition.
Jolly Roger: issued 1995, 3-1/2in (9cm), cast in resin, open edition.
House Call: issued 1995, 4in (10cm), cast in resin, open edition.
Friends: issued 1995, 1-3/4in (5cm), cast in resin, open edition.

77

LEFT to RIGHT:
77. **Splash:** issued 1995, 4in (10cm), cast in resin, open edition.
   Eddie Rickenbear: issued 1995, 3-1/2in (10cm), cast in resin, open edition.
   Dear Santa: issued 1995, 4in (10cm), cast in resin, open edition.
   Happy Bearday (Mini): issued 1995, 1-3/4in (5cm), cast in resin, open edition.

78

LEFT to RIGHT:
78. *Archibald:* issued 1995, 3in (8cm), cast in resin, open edition.
   First Mate: issued 1995, 3-3/4in (10cm), cast in resin, open edition.
   Tatters: issued 1995, 3in (8cm), cast in resin, open edition.
   Hucklebeary: issued 1995, 4in (10cm), cast in resin, open edition.

79

LEFT to RIGHT:
79. ***Baby on Board:*** issued 1995, 4-1/2in (11cm), cast in resin, open edition.
   Perfect Ten: issued 1995, 2-1/2in (6cm), cast in resin, open edition.
   First Step (Mini): issued 1995, 2-1/4in (5.65cm), cast in resin, open edition.
   Motherhood: issued 1995, 6in (15cm), cast in resin, open edition.

AGE COLLECTION

al paintings by Haddon Sundblom, a new collection of mantle ocking holders inspired by Cavanagh's popular line of Coca-ola® North Pole Bottling Works ornaments, as well as new addions to the Town Square Collection, Santa and Polar Bear figrines, musical and animation lines.

With each new year's entries, Cavanagh retires several imes increasing their value to collectors. Many of the earlier etired pieces now sell briskly in the secondary collector's market or several times their original price.

Cavanagh works hard all year to generate an increase in excitement for their Coca-Cola® Christmas collectibles. The Cavanagh Coca-Cola® Christmas Collectors Society began in 1993, with a membership certificate, newsletters, members-only ornaments and year-long special offers. In 1995, membership will exceed 20,000.

Building on the success of Cavanagh's Christmas collectibles, 1994 saw the introduction of the Coca-Cola® Heritage Collection, designed exclusively for gift and specialty stores. The 1995 line has been expanded from the first year's fifteen original Santa and Polar Bear figurines and musicals to include non-seasonal collectible times as well as introducing Cavanagh's first works based on the art of Norman Rockwell done for the Coca-Cola® Company.

The Coca-Cola® Polar Bears continue to be a major part of the Coca-Cola® Heritage collection. Without speaking a word, the lovable television stars from the current "Always Coca-Cola®" ad campaign have become popular favorites with consumers around the world.

Whimsical and charming Coca-Cola® Polar Bear figurines, snow globes, and musicals are all hand-painted and resin-sculpted, with die-struck brass medallions. Sculpting and the design, quality of the materials, and meticulous attention to detail are all in the tradition that marks the uncompromising Coca-Cola® commitment to excellence. Cavanagh Group International will continue to expand the Coca-Cola® Heritage Collection with respect for the past and care for aesthetics, authenticity, and craftsmanship. the Coca-Cola® Heritage Collection is based on the unmatched array of timeless images the Coca-Cola® company has created: from magazine advertising that ran almost 100 years ago to television commercials playing today.

Cavanagh will have introduced many millions of Americans to the exciting world of Coca-Cola® collectibles with an expanded line that now includes ornaments, figurines, snow globes, musicals, animations, and plush.

It all began in 1931 when the Coca-Cola® Company decided to expand its market with the concept that winter is just as good a time as summer to enjoy Coca-Cola®. The highly regarded illustrator, Haddon Sundblom, was commissioned to create the first painting of his version of Santa Claus. Sundblom's big, burly, fun-loving Santa debuted that year in the *Saturday Evening Post* and has appeared in advertising and on beverage cans and packaging over the past sixty plus Christmas seasons. These millions of advertising impressions have made the Coca-Cola® Santa the accepted image of Santa Claus in America. The foundation of Cavanagh's flagship line of collectible ornaments are based on those very masterpieces created by Haddon Sundblom.

In addition to the success of the Coca-Cola® Santa collection, Cavanagh's ornaments, figurines, and musicals depicting the Coca-Cola® Polar Bear have become an enormously popular part of the Cavanagh line. Inspired by the fun loving Coca-Cola® Polar Bear seen in television commercials around the globe, these whimsical Polar Bears are the instantly recognized television "stars" from the "Always Coca-Cola®" advertising campaign.

New ideas and products continue to place Cavanagh at the forefront of Coca-Cola® Christmas collectibles. 1994 releases include a new line of Santa on silk glass ornaments based on orig-

81

83

82

84

OPPOSITE PAGE:

80. *"Always Cool" Polar Bear (musical):* issued 1994, plays assortment of Coca-Cola® tunes, 11in (28cm), cast in resin, open limited edition.

81. *Eight Polar Bears:* issued 1994, 5in high by 11in long (13 x 28cm), cast in resin, limited edition 15000.

82. *Skating Polar Bear (Mini-musical):* issued 1994, plays tune "Always Coca-Cola®," 5in (13cm), cast in resin, limited edition.

83. *Polar Bear Family (musical):* issued 1995, plays tune "Always Coca-Cola®," 6-1/2in (16cm), cast in resin, open edition.

84. *Two Polar Bears on Ice (musical):* issued 1994, plays tune "Always Coca-Cola®," 5-1/2in (14cm), cast in resin, open edition.

CRYSTAL WORLD®

TEDDYLAND COLLECTION

Founded in 1983, Crystal World® has grown to become one of the most respected names in the world for production of 32% lead crystal collectibles. Their primary focus is on quality: quality of design, quality of materials and quality of workmanship. Couple this with their seemingly endless penchant for innovation, and it is easy to see why they are one of the largest crystal collectible producers in America.

Crystal World® draws on the talents of an international staff of accomplished designers: senior designer Ryuju Nakai, Tom Suzuki and Nocolo Mulargia. The uniqueness and originality of their designs have inspired countless collectors and admirers of fine crystal alike.

In 1986, Crystal World® introduced the innovative "Rainbow Castle." The "Rainbow Castle" was the first figurine to combine the shimmering beauty of clear faceted crystal with the magical rainbow-colored crystal of its mountain base. The result was an entirely new dimension in fine crystal collectibles which took the industry by storm. Crystal World®'s *Original Rainbow Castle Collection®* continues to be extremely popular.

Something else that sets this company apart from the others in the crystal figurine market is their finely detailed architectural collectibles. The "Empire State Building," the "Taj Mahal," the "Eiffel Tower" and the "U.S. Capitol Building" are a few of their limited edition works of art, each complete with a signed Certificate of Authenticity by the artist.

Among the most popular crystal figurines are Crystal World®'s whimsical *Teddyland* Collection and endearing *Collectible Kitties* collection, which are widely admired for their noted personality, warmth and charm.

86

87

88

89

OPPOSITE PAGE:
85. **Swinging Teddies:** issued 1991, 3in (8cm), crystal, open edition.

86. **Flower Teddy:** issued 1993, 1-1/2in (4cm), crystal, open edition.
87. **Small Loving Teddies:** issued 1990, 2in (5cm), crystal, open edition.
88. **Touring Teddies:** issued 1988, 2-1/8in (5.31cm), crystal, open edition.
89. **Happy Birthday Teddy:** issued 1989, 2in (5cm), crystal, open edition.

90

91

92

93

90. ***Beach Teddies:*** issued 1987, 2-1/8in (5.31cm), crystal, open edition.
91. ***Black Jack Teddies:*** issued 1993, 2in (5cm), crystal, open edition.
92. ***Gumball Teddy:*** issued 1991, 1-3/8in (3.9cm), crystal, open edition.
93. ***Patriotic Teddy:*** issued 1992, 3/4in (2cm), crystal, open edition.

94

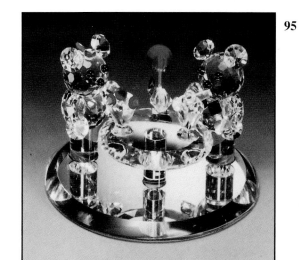

95

96

97

98

94. **Storytime Teddies:** issued 1990, 1-1/2in (4cm), crystal, open edition.
95. **Ice Cream Teddies:** issued 1992, 1-1/2in (4cm), crystal,
     open edition.
96. **Speedboat Teddies:** issued 1989, 2-1/2in (6cm), crystal, open edition.
97. **Teddy Family:** issued 1988, 1-1/2in (4cm), crystal, open edition.
98. **Santa Bear Christmas:** issued 1991, 2in (5cm), crystal, open edition.

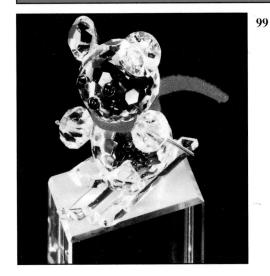

99

100

101

102

103

99. *Skiing Teddy:* issued 1987, 1-3/4in (5cm), crystal, open edition.
100. *Play it Again Ted:* issued 1991, 1-3/4in (5cm), crystal, open edition.
101. *Billiard Buddies:* issued 1992, 1-3/4in (5cm), crystal, open edition.
102. *Santa Bear Sleighride:* issued 1991, 1-1/2in (4cm), crystal,
open edition.
103. *Fly a Kite Teddy:* issued 1995, 1-3/4in (5cm), crystal, open edition.

104

105

106

104. **Sailing Teddies:** issued 1987, 3-1/4in (8.65cm),
     crystal, open edition.
105. **Teddy Bear Christmas:** issued 1987, 2in (5cm),
     crystal, open edition.
106. **Teddies at Eight:** issued 1987, 1-3/4in (5cm),
     crystal, open edition.

DEPARTMENT 56®

UPSTAIRS, DOWNSTAIRS BEARS™ COLLECTION

Department 56®, Inc., of Eden Prairie Minnesota, is a leading designer, importer and distributor of fine quality collectibles and other specialty giftware products in the United States. They began 19 years ago as a small department, number 56 in the Bachman's family owned nursery business. Today, they are a leader in the figurine segment of the giftware industry.

Department 56® was simply the number given to a new department for wholesale gift imports. The group began by importing fine Italian basketry. Then the original Snow Village, introduced in 1976, laid the groundwork for its collectibles lines.

This particular figurine was inspired by the warm, nostalgic image of a snow covered, turn-of-the-century town. The detailed ceramic houses were cheerfully lit and decorated for the Christmas season. Its Heritage Village Collection was introduced in 1984, beginning with the Dickens Village of porcelain shops. Other series followed, including the New England Village, Alpine Village, Little Town of Bethlehem, Christmas in the City and the North Pole Collection.

In addition to the villages, Department 56® introduced Snow Babies in 1986. These bisque porcelain figurines feature hand-painted faces and individually applied bisque crystals. They have become one of the most popular giftware collectibles in the United States.

In 1994, Department 56®, introduced the company's first line of Teddy Bear figurines called Upstairs, Downstairs Bears™, a collection of 32 figurines. The collection is inspired from original designs by Carol Lawson, a well-known English illustrator and author. Each piece is enchanting, hand-painted resin bears presented on mahogany bases with porcelain bottom stamps. The sizes of the figurines measure 3-1/2 to 6 inches. The Upstairs, Downstairs Bears™ have a classic furniture collection which consists of 6 pieces. Department 56® has plans to add new figurines to the collection in the near future.

UPSTAIRS BEARS™

The Upstairs Bears™ are the family of Mr. Frederick "Freddy" Pumphrey Bosworth whose great passion is his motor car. His wife, Henrietta, is always giving tea parties. Kitty, the eldest of the Bosworth children, is completely involved in talking and thinking of nothing but the Right Honorable Hugo "Binkie" Bartholomew to whom she is engaged. The twins, Henry and Alice, who are the middle children of the family, love to make mischief and do everything together, especially since the arrival of Baby Arthur, the youngest and sunniest bear in the Bosworth family. Named after his great-grandfather, Sir Arthur Pumphrey-Bartlett, he is the apple of everyone's eye and adored by all.

DOWNSTAIRS BEARS™

The Downstairs Bears™ "look after" the Bosworths. Baker, the butler, who is a bit straight-laced and stuffy, is in charge of the household. The cook, Mrs. Bumble rules the kitchen and is known for her delicious cakes and delectable pies. Nanny Mabold, in charge of the nursery, teaches tidiness, punctuality and, of course, proper manners. Flora Mardle, the Bosworth's parlour maid, helps Nanny in the nursery in addition to her duties at the many afternoon tea parties. Winston, employed as the footman and valet, in actuality is much more involved with attending to Freddy's motor car. And there is little Polly, the kitchen maid, youngest, smallest and shyest of the staff, who spends her afternoon going for a stroll in the park.

About the Artist:
CAROL LAWSON*

Carol Lawson was born in 1946 in the Yorkshire village of Giggleswick in northern England. She studied art at Harrogate College of Art – where she was awarded a First Class Honours degree in Art and Design. She then worked as an illustrator and married illustrator Chris McEwan in 1969. They lived in Paris for several years, illustrating children's books. In 1973, Carol and her husband returned to England and set up their own studio in Brighton. Carol has also designed doll house miniatures, porcelain figures, plates, and ornaments. Her hobbies include reading, gardening, tennis, and collecting old teddy bears, which she uses as models for Teddy Bear Characters.

In 1983, Carol and her husband moved to Newick, England, where they continue to live, write and illustrate. In 1986, she received a Gold Award from the Creative Circle Honours, an Award of Excellence from the 27th Design Annual Exhibition, and a commendation in the Campaign Press Advertising Awards. She has recently written and illustrated two children's books, *The Big Wish* and *The Sports Day.*

See Franklin Mint for other teddy bear figurine collections created by Carol Lawson.

107

107. ***Teddy Marchbanks:*** issued 1994, 4in (10cm), cast in resin, open edition.

108

109

110

111

112

OPPOSITE PAGE:
108. ***Mrs. Henrietta Bosworth:*** issued 1994, 6in (15cm), cast in resin, open edition.
   Baby Arthur Bosworth: issued 1994, 3-1/2in (9cm), cast in resin, open edition.
109. ***Mr. Bodicoat, Morning Delivery:*** issued 1994, 6-1/2in (16cm), cast in resin, open edition.
110. ***Mr. Frederick "Freddy," Pumphrey Bosworth:*** issued 1994, 6in (15cm), cast in resin, open edition.

111. ***Winston:*** issued 1994, 6-1/2in (16cm), cast in resin, open edition.
   Nanny Maybold: issued 1994, 6in (15cm), cast in resin, open edition.
   Barker, The Butler: issued 1994, 6-1/2in (16cm), cast in resin, open edition
112. ***Polly:*** issued 1994, 6-1/2in (16cm), cast in resin, open edition.
   Flora Mardle: issued 1994, 6in (15cm), cast in resin, open edition.

113

114

115

113. ***Alice Bosworth:*** issued 1994, 4in (10cm), cast in resin, open edition.
    Henry Bosworth: issued 1994, 4in (10cm), cast in resin, open edition.
    Kitty Bosworth: issued 1994, 5-1/2in (14cm), cast in resin, open edition.
114. ***Mrs. Bumble:*** issued 1994, 6-1/2in (16cm), cast in resin, open edition.
115. ***Nanny and Baby Arthur, Off to the Park:*** issued 1994,
    7 x 6-1/2in (18 x 16cm), cast in resin, open edition.

116

117

118

119

116. *Betsy Sweetcraft, Going Out For Tea:* issued 1994, 5-3/4in (15cm), cast in resin, open edition.
117. *Kitty and Binkie, Springtime Romance:* issued 1994, 4-1/2in (11cm), cast in resin, open edition.
118. *Henry and Alice Bosworth, The Easter Egg Hunt:* issued 1994, 5-1/2in (14cm), cast in resin, open edition.
119. *Miss Creedle, Time for Lessons:* issued 1994, 6-3/4in (17cm), cast in resin, open edition.

120

121

120. *Henry and Alice, Finding Treats:* issued 1995, 5-1/2in (14cm), cast in resin, open edition.
Alice Meeting the Christmas Fairy: issued 1995, 5in (13cm), cast in resin, open edition.
Kitty Cuts a Figure 8: issued 1995, 5-1/2in (14cm), cast in resin, open edition.
121. *Henry Brings Home the Presents:* issued 1995, 5-1/2in (14cm), cast in resin, open edition.
Henry and Alice, Building a Snowbear: issued 1995, 4-1/2in (11cm), cast in resin, open edition.

122

123

122. *Henry and Alice Hanging Garland:* issued 1995, 5-1/2in (14cm), cast in resin, open edition.
Nanny and Arthur Christmas Shopping: issued 1995, 6-3/4in (17cm), cast in resin, open edition.
123. *Henrietta Bosworth, The Easter Bonnet:* issued 1994, 7in (18cm), cast in resin, open edition.
Freddy Bosworth, Ready for a Spin: issued 1994, 6-3/4in (17cm), cast in resin, open edition.
Polly, Spring Flowers: issued 1994, 5-1/2in (14cm), cast in resin, open edition.

124

125

126

124. *Henrietta's Tea Party:* issued 1994, 5in (13cm), cast in resin, limited edition 5,600 pieces, open edition.

125. *Daphne Bonnett, Pretty As A Picture:* issued 1994, 3-3/4in (10cm), cast in resin, open edition.

126. *Flora Mardle the Artist:* issued 1994, 6in (15cm), cast in resin, open edition.

ENESCO® CORPORATION

Enesco® Corporation, a producer of fine giftware, collectibles and home decor accessories, is one of the most respected names in the giftware industry. The Company has been regarded as a leader in its field for 35 years. Credited with being among the most innovative and trendsetting designers and producers of fine gifts and collectibles, Enesco® continues its steady growth and prominence worldwide. The Company was founded in 1958 as a division of N. Shure Company. Following the sale of N. Shure, the import division reorganized as Enesco®, formed from the phonic spellings of the prior parent company name initials --NS Co. Originally based in Chicago, Enesco® relocated its corporate offices to Elk Grove Village in 1975 and to Itasca in 1995. The Company's showroom, warehouse and distribution facility remain in Elk Grove Village. The Company also operates the Enesco® Worldwide Giftware group with wholly owned subsidiaries in Canada, Great Britain, Germany, Scotland, and Hong Kong as well as a network of exclusive distributors strategically located throughout the world.

The Enesco® product line includes more than 12,000 giftware, collectible and home decor items and is divided into three divisions: Enesco® Designed Giftware, Enesco® Gift Gallery and International Collections.

The Enesco® Designed Giftware Division is responsible for the award-winning Enesco® Precious Moments Collection, one of the most popular collectibles in the World, Enesco® Treasury of Christmas Ornaments, Sisters and Best Friends, Sesame Street Giftware, Lucy & Me®, Chapeau Noelle™, and Gnomes product lines. The Enesco® Gift Gallery division includes general giftware and collectibles such as the award winning Cherished Teddies® Collection, Enesco® Small World of Music Collection, Memories of Yesterday, Laura's Attic, from Barbie® with Love, Mickey and Co. Disney® Giftware, Calico Kittens™, Mary's Moo-Moos, Star Trek, Elvis Presley and Beatles product lines.

In 1994 Enesco® created International Collections, a new division, to market several newly acquired companies. Under the International Collections umbrellas, Enesco® operates Otagiri, a home accent company, Via Vermont, a designer and producer of fine art glass giftware, Border Fine Arts, a United Kingdom-based manufacturer of collectible animal sculptures and Lilliput Lane, the United Kingdom-based manufacturer of vernacular architectural cottages. Each of the above named companies is now an ownership affiliated operating company of Enesco®.

More than 75 percent of Enesco®'s products are designed by the company's staff of 60 artists and designers. The company also markets licensed gifts and collectibles from well-known artists such as, Priscilla Hillman (Calico Kittens™ and Cherished Teddies®), Ellen Williams (Sisters and Best Friends), Lucy Rigg (Lucy & Me®, and Chapeau Noelle™) Lesley Ann Ivory (Ivory Cats), Kathy Wise, Peter Fagan (Centimental Bears and PennyWhistle Lane) and brand name companies including Coca-Cola®, Dodge, Ford, Chevrolet, Sega, and McDonald®'s.

Enesco® is known for its great quality and records in the collectible market. The company has produced some of the most popular teddy bear figurine collections in the industry – Collections such as Cherished Teddies®, Lucy & Me®, Chapeau Noelle™, PennyWhistle Lane and Centimental Bears. Each collection has a unique style and interest to the collector.

Enesco® Corporation plans to continue bringing collectors many years of enjoyment in collecting teddy bear figurines.

CHERISHED TEDDIES® COLLECTION

Fall of 1991, Enesco® introduced Cherished Teddies® Collection of teddy bear figurines. The first 16 figurines began appearing in retail stores in Spring 1992. Today there are many single and multiple figurines in the collection, which is sold and known throughout the world.

Each teddy bear figurine is sculptured in cold-cast resin. The detailed figurines come with a name, title and a Certificate of Adoption so that collectors can officially "adopt" the teddy bears. To date, more than 100,000 collectors have registered their teddy bears with Enesco®'s "Adoption Center." Cherished Teddies® celebrate the seasons, special occasions, holidays, and important personal events.

The collection is based on illustrations by artist and children's author Priscilla Hillman. In the late 1980's, she sketched cute and cuddly teddy bears and submitted her drawings to Enesco®, where they transformed her illustrations into three-dimensional figurines.

Since its debut, the collection has received worldwide recognition from collectors and the collectibles industry. Within its first year, the figurine "Old Friends Are The Best Friends" won a 1992 TOBY® Award. The figurine "Friends Are Never Far Apart" won a Collector Editions 1992 Award of Excellence in the musicals under $100 category. "Friends Come in All Sizes" received a 1992 Giftware Association Award in the Tabletop and Collectibles category in England. The catalog group Retail Resources Inc. named the collection the 1992 Most Outstanding New Product. Also in 1992, Stanhome Inc. Enesco®'s parent company named Cherished Teddies® Product of the Year.

In 1993, NALED (National Association of Limited Edition Dealers), named Cherished Teddies® Collectible of the Year, a prestigious honor in only its first year of eligibility for the award, and named Priscilla Hillman second runner up for Artist of the Year. Also in 1993, Parkwest named the Cherished Teddies® Collection the Outstanding New Product Line and named Priscilla Hillman the Outstanding New Artist; and "Friendship Weathers All Storms" won an Award of Excellence from Collector Editions. Retail Resource Inc. named Cherished Teddies® Best New Product and Best Figurine. Three Cherished Teddies® were nominated for a 1993 TOBY® Award. In 1994, NALED (National Association of Limited Edition Dealers) named Priscilla Hillman Artist of the Year; the musical "Friendship Weathers All Storms" was named Musical of the Year first runner up; and the ornament "Alice" was honored as Ornament of the Year second runner up. "Our Cherished Family" was recognized internationally by the Florence Gift Mart in Italy. Parkwest awarded the Cherished Teddies® nativity scene as the Most Outstanding Nativity and Retail Resources Inc., named "Blossom and Beth", the Most Outstanding Figurine for 1994. In 1994 Canadian Collectibles of the Year Awards, presented the collection with the Collectibles of the Year Award for figurines under $75.

In response to the overwhelming collector enthusiasm for the award-winning collection, Enesco® introduced a Cherished Teddies® Club in 1994. The Charter Year began January 1, 1995. The club has become Enesco®'s fastest growing club.

The Cherished Teddies® Collection is ranked among the top ten collectibles by giftware market research listings. The collection includes plush, articulated bears and gift accessories, including Post-it™ notes, mini plates, waterfalls, ornaments and musical figurines. These adorable teddy bear figurines have found a special place in the hearts of collectors with their warm expressions and universal appeal.

Enesco® Corporation plans to introduce new Cherished Teddies® characters to the figurine collection.

127. ***Theodore, Samantha and Tyler, "Friends Come In All Sizes":*** won the 1992 England Giftware Association Award, issued 1992, 2-3/4in (7cm), cast in resin, open edition.

CHERISHED TEDDIES® COLLECTOR'S CLUB

Enesco® Corporation recently announced that they have signed more than 40,000 members to the newly created Cherished Teddies® Collector's Club, making it the fastest growing club in Enesco® History. The Club's Charter Year officially began January 1, 1995.

The club was formed in response to the overwhelming collector enthusiasm for the award winning Cherished Teddies® Collections.

The club gives collectors the opportunity to become Charter Members and enjoy the benefits of being a Bearafactor to the bears who come from the Cherished Teddies® Town, the village where the Club bears reside. The annual membership fee is $17.50, bearafactors receive the limited edition figurine and "spokesbear" Cub E. Bear; a welcome letter from club headquarters; a certificate of Charter Year Membership; a key to Cherished Teddies® Town lapel pin; a subscription to *The Town Tattler*, the official town newspaper; the opportunity to purchase two Members Only Figurines during 1995; the Town Mayor Wilson T. Beary and Town Registrar Hilary Hugabear and decorative easel to display behind the club bears.

127

About the Artist:
PRISCILLA HILLMAN

Priscilla Hillman has endearing and special childhood memories of writing with her sister at the kitchen table with paint brushes. Watercolors have influenced her charming illustrations and uplifting children's books that have touched the hearts of both young and old.

Art was always a central part of Priscilla's life. Although she loved drawing, Priscilla decided to study botany at the University of Rhode Island. After graduating, she worked for the U.S. Oceanographic Office but continued pursuing her artistic interest.

"Tumpy Rumple," her first effort at illustrating and writing a children's book, took her three years to complete. Priscilla then created "Precious Bears," which appeared on needlecraft and greeting cards.

In the late 1980s, a serious back problem kept Priscilla inactive for several months. During this time, Priscilla "drew in her mind." When she was finally able to move about, Priscilla went straight to her drawing board to put "sketches" of cute and cuddly teddy bears on paper. The Cherished Teddies® Collection came to life, and Priscilla's first giftware collection based on her charming illustrations was introduced in 1992. The Cherished Teddies® Collection has since received worldwide recognition from collectors and the collectibles industry, as some of the figurines have won prestigious awards of excellence.

With the success of the Cherished Teddies® Collection, Enesco introduced another collection by Priscilla Hillman in 1993. The Calico Kittens™ Collection features adorable cold cast cat figurines with messages of friendship and love.

128

129

130

128. *Heidi and David, "Special Friends":* issued 1993, 2-3/4in (7cm), cast in resin, open edition.

129. Blossom and Beth, *"Friends Are Never Far Apart":* musical tune "Let Me Be Your Teddy Bear", won 1992 Collector's Edition Award; issued 1992, 7-1/2in (19cm), cast in resin, open editions.

130. *Theodore, Samantha and Tyler, "Friendship Weathers All Storms":* issued 1993, 2-3/4in (7cm), cast in resin, open edition.

51

131

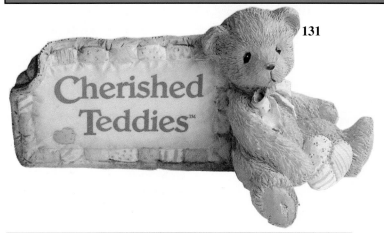

132

133

134

135

136

131. *Cherished Teddies Signage Plaque:* issued 1992, 2-1/2in (6cm), cast in resin, open edition.
132. *Joshua, "Love Rapairs All"*
133. *Jonathan, "Sail with Me"; Harrison, "We're Going Places"; Thomas, "Chuggin' Along":* issued 1993, 3in (8cm), cast in resin, open edition.
134. *Zachary, "Yesterday's Memories Are Today's Treasurers":* issued 1992, 3-1/2in (9cm), cast in resin, open edition.
135. *Jacki, "Hugs and Kisses; Sara, "Love Ya"; Karen, "Best Buddy:* issued 1992, 3in (8cm), cast in resin, open edition.
136. *Robbie and Rachel, "Love Bears All Things":* issued 1993, 3in (8cm), cast in resin, open edition.

158

160

159

162

161

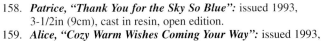

163

158. *Patrice, "Thank You for the Sky So Blue":* issued 1993,
3-1/2in (9cm), cast in resin, open edition.

159. *Alice, "Cozy Warm Wishes Coming Your Way":* issued 1993,
4in (10cm), cast in resin, issued only for 1993 year.

160. *Douglas, "Let's be Friends":* issued 1992, 3-1/2in (9cm),
cast in resin, retired 1995.

161. *Charlie, "The Spirit of Friendship Warms The Heart":* issued
1992, 3-1/2in (9cm), cast in resin, open edition.

162. *"Thank You for a Friend That's True":* musical tune: *"Jesus Loves
Me,"* issued 1993, 4-1/2in (11cm), cast in resin on wooden base,
open edition.

163. *Carolyn, "Wishing You All Good Things":* issued 1993,
3in (8cm), cast in resin, open edition.

57

164

165

166

164. **Left to Right:** *Angie, "I Brought The Star":* 3-1/2in (9cm); Creche with Coverlet: 8in (20cm), wood resin, fabric; **Mary, Baby and Joseph, "A Baby Is God's Gift of Love":** 3in (cm); all issued 1992, figurines cast in resin, open edition.
165. **Left to Right:** *Richard with Camel, "My Gift Is Loving"; Edward with Donkey, "My Gift is Caring"; Wilbur with Teddy, "My Gift Is Sharing":* issued 1992, 3-1/2in (9cm), cast in resin, open edition.
166. **Left to Right:** *"Friendship Pulls Us Through"; "Ewe Make Being Friends Special":* issued 1993, 5in (13cm), cast in resin, open edition.

167. *"Cherish The King":* musical tune: "Oh, Little Town of Bethlehem," issued 1993, 6in (15cm), cast in resin/wooden base, open edition.

168. *Beth, "Happy Holidays, Deer Freind":* issued 1992, 4in (10cm), cast in resin, open edition.

169. *"Friends Like You Are Precious and True":* issued 1993, 5in (13cm), cast in resin, open edition.

170. *Sammy, "Little Lambs Are In My Care":* issued 1992, 4in (10cm), cast in resin, open edition.

171. *Steven, "A Season Filled with Sweetness":* issued 1992, 3in (8cm), cast in resin, open edition.

172

173

174

175

176

172. **Left to Right: *Buckey and Brenda, "How I Love Being Friends with You":*** issued 1993, 3in (8cm), cast in resin, open edition.

173. ***Gary, "True Friendships Are Scarce":*** issued 1993, 3-3/4in (10cm), cast in resin, open edition.

174. ***Prudence, "A Friend to Be Thankful For":*** issued 1993 3in (8cm), cast in resin, open edition.

175. ***Theodore, Samantha and Tyler "Friends Come In All Sizes":*** issued 1992, 9in (23cm), cast in resin, open edition.

176. ***Gretel, "We Make Magic, Me and You":*** issued 1993, 4in (10cm), cast in resin, open edition.

177

178

179

180

181

182

184

183

185

177. **Left to Right:** *Tom, Tom the Piper's Son, "Wherever You Go, I'll Follow";*
Little Jack Horner, "I'm Plum Happy You're My Friend": issued 1994,
3-1/2in (9cm), cast in resin, open edition.
178. *Jack and Jill, "Our Friendship Will Never Tumble":* issued 1994, 3-1/2 in (9cm),
cast in resin, open edition.
179. *Baby, "Cradled with Love":* issued 1993, 3in (8cm), cast in resin, open edition.
180. *"Beary Special One",* Age 1: issued 1993, 2-1/2in (6cm), cast in resin, open edition.
181. **Left to Right:** *Little Miss Muffet, "I'm Never Afraid with You at My Side"; Little Bo*
Peep, "Looking for a Friend Like You": issued 1994, 3-1/2in (9cm), cast in resin.
182. *"Chalking Up Six Wishes",* Age 6: issued 1993, 3in (8cm), cast in resin, open edition.
183. *"Three Cheers for You",* Age 3: issued 1993, 3in (8cm), cast in resin, open edition.
184. *"Two Sweet Two Bear",* Age 2: issued 1993, 2-1/2in (6cm), cast in resin, open edition.
185. *Mary, Mary Quite Contrary, "Friendship Blooms with Loving Care":*
issued 1994, 4in (10cm), cast in resin, open edition.

186

187

188

189

190

191

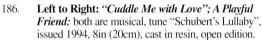

186.   **Left to Right:** *"Cuddle Me with Love"; A Playful Friend:* both are musical, tune "Schubert's Lullaby", issued 1994, 8in (20cm), cast in resin, open edition.
187.   *"Unfolding Happy Wishes for You"*, Age 4: issued 1993, 3in (8cm), cast in resin, open edition. *"Color Me Five"* Age 5: issued 1993, 3in (8cm), cast in resin, open edition.
188.   *Betty, "Bubblin' Over with Love":* issued 1994, 2-3/4in (7cm), cast in resin, open edition.
189.   *Christopher, "Old Friends Are The Best Friends":* musical tune "My Favorite Things", 3-1/2 in (9cm); *Katie, "A Friend Always Knows When You Need a Hug":* musical tune "Wind Beneath My Wings", 5in (13cm); both issued 1994, cast in resin/wooden base, open edition.
190.   *My Favorite Things, "A Cuddle and You"*; musical tune "My Favorite Things," issued 1994, 12-1/2in (32cm), cast in resin, open edition.
191.   *Smooth Sailing:* musical tune "Love Will Keep Us Together", issued 1994, 8in (20cm), cast in resin, open edition.

192

193

194

195

196

197

192. **Left to Right:** *Billy, "Everyone Needs a Cuddle"; Betsey "The First Step to Love":* 4in (10 cm); *Bobbie, A Little Friendship to Share:* 2-1/2in (6cm); issued 1994, cast in resin, open edition.

193. *Patience, "Happiness Is Home Made":* issued 1994, 2in (5cm), cast in resin, open edition.

194. *Tracie and Nicole, "Side By Side with Friends":* issued 1993, 4-1/2in (11cm), cast in resin, open edition.

195. *Taylor, "Sail The Seas with Me":* issued 1994, 3in (8cm), cast in resin, open edition.

196. *Wyatt, "I'm Called Little Running Bear":* issued 1994, 3-1/2in (9cm), cast in resin, open edition.

197. *Jedediah, "Giving Thanks for Friends":* 4in (10cm); *Thanksgiving Quilt Me:* 2in (5cm), issued 1994, cast in resin, open edition.

198

199

200

201

202

203

204

198.   *Stacie, "You Lift My Spirit":* issued 1994, 3-3/4in (10cm), cast in resin, open edition.

199.   **Left to Right:** *Winona, "Fair Feather Friends"; Willie, "Bears of a Feather Stay Together":* issued 1994, both are 3in (8cm), cast in resin, open edition.

200.   **Left to Right:** *Phoebe, "A Little Friendship Is a Big Blessing":* 2-1/2in (6cm); *Wylie, "I'm Called Little Friend":* 3in (8cm), issued 1994, cast in resin, open edition.

201.   *Eric, "Bear Tidings of Joy":* issued 1994, 4-1/2in (11cm), cast in resin, open edition.

202.   *Nils, "Near and Deer for Christmas":* issued 1994, 4in (10cm), cast in resin, open edition.

203.   *Jacob Bearly, "You Will Be Haunted by Three Spirits":* issued 1994, 3-1/2in (9cm), cast in resin, open edition.

204.   *Gloria, "I am the Ghost of Christmas Past"; Garland, "I am the Ghost of Christmas Present"; Gabriel, "I am the Ghost of Christmas Yet to Come":* issued 1994, 3-1/2in (9cm), cast in resin, open edition.

223

224

225

226

227

223. **Top:** *Madeline, "A Cup Full of Cheer"*; **Middle:** *Margaret, "A Cup Full of Love"*; **Bottom:** *Marilyn, "A Cup Full of Friendship":* issued 1995, all 3in (8cm), cast in resin, open edition.

224. *Priscilla and Greta, "Our Hearts Belong to You":* issued 1995, 3in (8cm), cast in resin, limited edition 19,950, open.

225. *"AuClaire DeLune":* musical, issued 1995, 5in (13cm), cast in resin, open edition.

226. **Left to Right:** *Carrie, "The Future 'Beneath' All Things":* 2-3/4in (7cm); *Bea, "Bee My Friend":* 3-3/4in (10cm); both issued 1995, cast in resin, open edition.

227. *Connie, "You're A Sweet Treat":* issued 1994; *Breanna, "Pumpkin Patch Pals":* issued 1994, 3in (8cm), cast in resin, open edition.

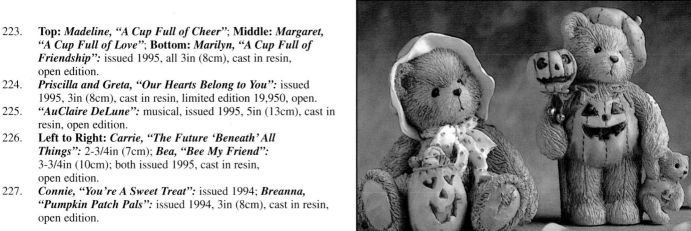

228

229

230

231

228. **Left to Right:** *Yule, "Building a Sturdy Friendship":* 3in (8cm); *Ginger, "Painting Your Holidays with Love":* 3-1/8in (8.31cm); *Meri, "Handsewn Holidays":* 3-1/4in (8.65cm); all issued 1995, cast in resin, open edition.

229. **Left to Right:** *Mary, "A Special Friend Warms The Season":* issued 1993; *Earl, Warm Hearted Friends":* issued 1995, 4in (10cm), cast in resin, open edition.

230. **Left to Right:** *Nicholas, "You're at the Top of My List":* 4in (10cm); *Holly, "A Cup of Homemade Love":* 3-3/4in (10cm); both issued 1995.

231. *Pat, "Falling for You":* issued 1995, 3-1/2in (10cm), cast in resin, open edition.

About the Artist:
LUCY RIGG

Lucy Rigg began making baker's clay teddy bear figurines in 1969 while awaiting the birth of her daughter, Noelle. She decorated the nursery with her first teddy bears. Friends and family were so enchanted with the original creations that Lucy began making them for others.

Teddy bear collectors bought her hand painted clay dough bears, known as "Rigglets," at street fairs. To keep up with the growing demand, she imposed a quota on herself to make 100 teddy bears per day and often stayed up until the wee hours of the morning to meet her goal.

As her teddy bears became more popular, Lucy formed her own company. In the late 1970's Enesco Corporation proposed turning Lucy's handmade teddy bears into a line of porcelain bisque figurines and accessories. The figurines produced in 1979 had the name "Rigglets" printed on the bottom of them. In 1980, Enesco® dropped the name Rigglets and began using "Lucy & Me®" as the official name. Since Enesco® introduced the Lucy & Me® collection in 1979, the collection has received steady support from collectors and teddy bear lovers. New collectors of Lucy & Me® see small, detailed teddy bears dressed up as celebrities and professionals, celebrating traditional and contemporary occasions.

The Lucy & Me® collection has earned artist Lucy Rigg the loyalty and love of collectors all across the world who thrive on the heartfelt care she bestows on each of her figurines. The newest line features a bear for every occasion from the standard birthday, wedding, and anniversary to a ballet recital and a good report card. Other new pieces are a Statue of Liberty, a bingo player, and a male and female square dancers. Collectors can relate to the sweet little bears in this line. There is hardly an event, occasion or theme Lucy & Me® figurines do not honor!

Whether you discovered the collection of figurines in 1971 or in the 1990's, no one can argue that the Lucy & Me® collection is a "hit" with collectors, young and old.

Enesco introduced in 1994, another sensational teddy bear line by Lucy called Chapeau Noelle™, a limited edition collection of porcelain teddy bears wearing exquisite hats. This collection was inspired by the artist's love for hats and her love for her daughter Noelle. The figurines are limited to editions of 2000 and come with a Certificate of Authenticity that includes both Lucy Rigg's and Noelle Rigg's stamped signature as well as the bear's name. Each wears a hat. Porcelain bisque figurines measure 5 inches high.

There is also a collection called Chapeau Noelle™ Petite. Limited to editions of 5000 each, these figurines measure 3 inches high. Lucy names many of her bears after friends, family and historical figures who had an influence on her life. Bears in both collections come in a specially designed Chapeau Noelle™ gift box.

Lucy Rigg continues to operate Lucy and Company, designing diaries, baby announcements, calendars and her "teddy bear" version of popular children books. Lucy has been a teddy bear collector herself since 1968. Her Seattle home is filled with toys and collectibles, which project the warmth and joy of her artwork. She has created a special room to display the Lucy & Me® collection, which includes several hundred figurines, plus many accessory items each adorned with her loveable teddy bears. Lucy Rigg is known today as one of the most prolific teddy bear artists in the world.

Note: All 1979 production was stamped "Rigglets" on bottom of figurine.

232. **Left to Right:**
Oak Leaf;
Hazelnut;
Maple Leaf:
issued 1991,
open edition all
bears measure
2-1/2in (6cm),
cast in porcelain bisque.

232

233

234

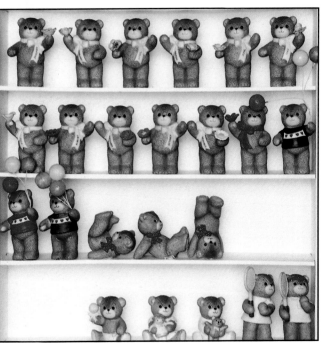

235

LEFT to RIGHT:

233. Top Row: *4 bears with red bows; 3 bears with shirts:* issued 1979, retired 1989.**Second Row:** *Bear with shirt:* issued 1979, retired 1989, *2 Couples with Red Bows:* issued 1979, retired 1989; *2 bears with Indoor Plants:* issued 1979, retired 1985, *Bride and Groom:* issued 1979, open edition. **Third Row:** *World's Greatest Dad:* issued 1979, retired 1986, *Football Player:* issued 1979, open edition, *Bear with Birthday Prop/The Present:* issued 1979, retired 1986, *Basketball Player; Baseball Player; Soccer Player:* issued 1979, open edition. **Bottom Row:** *Bear with Birthday Prop/Cake:* issued 1979, retired 1986, *2 Moms Hugging Cubs:* issued 1979, retired 1988, *Doctor and Nurse:* issued 1979, retired 1990, *Bear in Irish Suit:* issued 1979, retired 1985.

234. Top Row: *Couple with "I Love You" Hearts:* issued 1981, retired 1988, *2 Bears Kissing with Hearts:* issued 1981, retired 1989, *Professor:* issued 1981, retired 1986, *Business Man; Cowboy:* issued 1981, retired 1985. **Second Row:** *Girl/Boy Graduates:* issued 1981, open edition, *Hairdresser; Dentist:* issued 1981, retired 1985. **Third Row:** *Age 1 Bear/Girl:* issued 1982, retired 1989, *Age 1 Bear/Boy:* issued 1982, open edition, *Age 2 Bear/Girl:* issued 1982, retired 1989, *Age 2 Bear/Boy:* issued 1982, open edition, *Age 3 Bear/Girl:* issued 1982, retired 1989, *Age 3 Bear/Girl:* issued 1982, open edition. **Bottom Row:** *Age 4 Bear/Boy:* issued 1982, open edition, *Age 4 Bear/Girl:* issued 1982, retired 1989, *Age 5 Bear/Boy:* issued 1982, open edition, *Age 5 Bear/Girl:* issued 1982, retired 1989, *Age 6 Bear/Girl:* issued 1982, retired 1989, *Age 6 Bear/Boy:* issued 1982, open edition.

235.   **Top Row:** *January Bear; February Bear; March Bear; April Bear; May Bear; June Bear:* issued 1982, retired 1987. **Second Row:** *July Bear; August Bear; September Bear; October Bear; November Bear; December Bear:* issued 1982, retired 1987, *Bear with Balloons/Blue Shirt:* issued 1982, retired 1989. **Third Row:** *Bear with Balloons/Red Shirt; Bear with Balloons/Green Shirt:* issued 1982, retired 1989, *3 Tumbling Bears Wearing Red Bows:* issued 1982, retired 1990. **Bottom Row:** *3 Babies Sitting with Toys:* issued 1982, retired 1990, *2 Tennis Players:* issued 1982, retired 1989.

All bears measure 3 – 3-1/2in (8 – 9cm), cast in porcelain bisque.

248

250

249

LEFT to RIGHT:

248.   **Top Row:** *Baby on Goose:* issued 1987, retired 1990, *2 Birthday Clowns:* issued 1988, retired 1990, *Candy Corn; Indian Corn; Dragon:* issued 1989, open edition, *Gardener Inside Flower Pot:* issued 1989, retired 1992. **Second Row:** *4 Bears Dressed as Flowers:* issued 1989, open edition, *3 tumbling bears in bunny ears:* issued 1989, retired 1992. **Third Row:** *Boy/Girl "Prisoners of Love":* issued 1989, open edition, *Gangster; Flapper:* issued 1989, retired 1991, *Girl with Box of Roses; Boy Playing a Guitar:* issued 1989, retired 1992, *"1990" Boy with Box of Candy and Roses:* issued 1990, retired 1990. **Bottom Row:** *Bear Dressed as Box of Candy; Bear Dressed as Rose:* issued 1989, retired 1992, *Irishman with Kisses on Face; Bear Dressed as Pot of Gold; Bear Dressed as Blarney Stone; Boy with Flat of Flowers:* issued 1989, retired 1992, *Bear Dressed as a Cheeseburger:* issued 1989, open edition.

249.   **Top Row:** *"For Teacher" Bear Dressed as Apple:* issued 1988, open edition, *Crossing Guard:* issued 1989, retired 1992, *Pregnant Mom Eating Ice Cream:* issued 1989, retired 1991, *Lamaze Couple:* issued 1989, retired 1993, *50's Boy in Letterman's Sweater:* issued 1989, retired 1992. **Second Row:** *Bear Dressed as Pig:* issued 1989, retired 1991, *Bear Dressed as Chicken:* issued 1989, open edition, *Bear Dressed as Milkshake:* issued 1989, retired 1993, *2 Birthday Clowns:* issued 1988, retired 1990, *Bear Dressed as French Fries:* issued 1989, open edition,

Bear Dressed as Cow: issued 1989, retired 1992. **Third Row:** *Fairy Godmother; Cinderella in Ball Gown; Prince with Glass Slipper:* issued 1989, retired 1991, *Cinderella Dressed in Rags:* issued 1989, retired 1990, *Girl Old-Fashioned Golfer:* issued 1989, retired 1992, *Boy Old-"Fashioned Golfer:* issued 1989, retired 1993. **Bottom Row:** *Courageous Lion; Tin Man; Scarecrow:* issued 1989, retired 1993, *Dorothy and Toto:* issued 1989, retired 1992, all part of a *Wizard of Oz Series; Charlie Chaplin; Rhette and Scarlett:* issued 1989, retired 1991.

250.   **Top Row:** *Bear Bathing in Bubbly Tub:* issued 1989, retired 1991, *Jack and Jill:* issued 1989, open edition, *Mother Goose:* issued 1989, retired 1991, *Little Miss Muffet:* issued 1989, retired 1991. **Second Row:** *Devil; Bat:* issued 1990, retired 1993, *Bear Dressed as Strawberry:* issued 1989, retired 1991, *Baseball Player; Quarterback #17; Hockey Player #17; Surfer Bear:* issued 1989, retired 1993. **Third Row:** *Indian Girl/Boy:* issued 1990, open edition, *Cowboy; Cowgirl; Boy/Girl Cavebear:* issued 1990, retired 1993, *Bear Dressed as Cornucopia:* issued 1990, open edition. **Bottom Row:** *Mail Carrier; Bear Dressed as Trick-or-Treat Bag:* issued 1990, open edition, *Maid/Butler; Bear Dressed as Ice Cream Cone:* issued 1990, retired 1993, *Fireman:* issued 1990, open edition, *Girl/Boy Tennis Players:* issued 1990, retired 1993.

All bears measure 2-1/2 – 3in (6 – 8cm), cast in porcelain bisque.

251

252

253

LEFT to RIGHT:

251.   **Top Row:** *Ladybug:* issued 1990, open edition, *Barrel of Vegetables; Seed Packet; Radish:* issued 1990, retired 1993; *Bear Dressed as an Easter Basket; Noah's Ark Lion:* issued 1990, open edition. **Second Row:** *Bear Dressed as Fortune Cookie:* issued 1990, retired 1992, *3 Bears in Diapers and Bunny Ears:* issued 1990, open edition, *Girl Dressed in Easter Clothes:* issued 1990, retired 1992, *Bear Dressed as Chick in an Egg:* issued 1990, retired 1993, *Honey Bee:* issued 1990, open edition. **Third Row:** *Noah's Wife; Noah:* issued 1990, open edition, *Bear Dressed as Sheep; Bear Dressed as Donkey:* issued 1990, retired 1992, *Bear Dressed as Taco:* issued 1990, retired 1993, *Bear Dressed as Chinese Take-Out Food:* issued 1990, open edition. **Bottom Row:** *Noah's Ark Toucan; Noah's Ark Giraffe:* issued 1990, open edition, *Noah's Ark Turtle:* issued 1990, retired 1993, *Noah's Ark Tiger; Noah's Ark Zebra; Noah's Ark Monkey; Noah's Ark Elephant:* issued 1990, open edition. All bears measure 2-1/2 – 3in (6 – 8cm), cast in porcelain bisque.

252.   **Top Row:** *Peter Pan; Captain Hook; Marilyn Monroe; Basketball Player #23; Soccer Player; Wicked Witch of the West (Wizard of Oz):* issued 1990, retired 1993, *Sweet Sixteen Girl:* issues 1990, retired 1992. **Second Row:** *Little Bo Peep:* issued 1990, retired 1993, *Tom Tom The Piper's Son:* issued 1990, retired 1992, *Mermaid; Crocodile with Clock; Tinkerbell; Wendy:* issued 1990, retired 1993. **Bottom Row:** *Pilgrim Girl/Boy:* issued 1990, open edition, *Mary Poppins:* issued 1990, retired 1992, *Elvis Presley:* issued 1990, open edition, *Bear Dressed as Green Pepper; Bear Dressed Mushroom:* issued 1990, retired 1992. All bears measure 2-1/2in (6cm), cast in porcelain bisque.

253.   **Top Row:** *Bear Holding Candle:* issued 1979, retired 1983, *2 Bears Kissing Holding Presents:* issued 1979, retired 1989, *Couple Hugging Each Other:* issued 1979, retired 1987. **Second Row:** *2 Carolers with Cat:* issued 1979, retired 1982, *2 Bears Standing Next to Snowbears:* issued 1979, retired 1982. **Third Row:** *2 Candle Climbers - Teddy/Angel; Santa with Toy Bag; Mrs. Claus with Cookie Tray; Bear with Drum:* issued 1979, retired 1985. **Bottom Row:** *Mrs. Claus with Present; Santa with Toy Bag; 3 Choir Bears:* issued 1979, retired 1985. All bears measure 3in (8cm), cast in porcelain bisque.

254

255

256

LEFT to RIGHT:

254. **Top Row:** *Dad; Mom; Grandpa; Grandma:* issued 1982, retired 1989, *2 Skiers:* issued 1982, retired 1986. **Second Row:** *(Large) Violin Player; Caroler; Trumpeter:* issued 1983, retired 1986, *Large Boy (Bobby) Pulling Girl (Noelle) on Sled:* issued 1983, retired 1987. **Third Row:** *2 Skaters; (small) Violin Player, Caroler; Bear Mailing Letter to Santa; Girl Holding Teddy and Package:* issued 1983, retired 1986. **Bottom Row:** *Boy Pulling Girl on Sled:* issued 1983, retired 1989, *Bear Making Snowman; 2 Skiers:* issued 1983, retired 1986, *Santa with Toy Bag:* issued 1984, retired 1985. All bears measure 2-1/2 – 3-1/2in (6 – 9cm), cast in porcelain bisque.

255. **Top Row:** *4 Bears Holding Christmas Toys:* issued 1984, retired 1989. **Second Row:** *6 Piece set - Family Decorating Christmas Tree:* issued 1984, retired 1989. **Third Row:** *Three Tumbling Santas:* issued 1985, retired 1989; *Dad Sitting in Chair Reading to Son:* issued 1985, retired 1987. **Bottom Row:** *"Our 1st Christmas Together" Couple with Mistletoe:* issued 1985, retired 1985, *Girl Kneeling Next Cradle; Girl Kneeling Next to Doll House; Santa with List:* issued 1985, retired 1989. All bears measure 2-1/2 – 3-1/2in (6 – 9cm), cast in porcelain bisque.

256. **Top Row:** *3 Elves with Toys and Work Bench:* issued 1985, retired 1989, *Bear in Sleigh:* issued 1985, retired 1986. **Second Row:** *4 Bears Holding Tree, Flowers, Candle, Candy Cane:* issued 1985, retired 1989, *Girl Opening Present with Teddy:* issued 1985, retired 1988, *Bear Wearing Cookie Cutters on Feet:* issued 1985, retired 1987. **Third Row:** *4 Bears Holding Christmas Props:* issued 1985, retired 1988, *3 Bears Riding on Sled:* issued 1986, open edition. **Bottom Row:** *Three Wise Men Bearing Gifts:* issued 1986, retired 1990, *December Bear:* issued 1985, retired 1990, *Joseph/Baby Jesus/Mary:* issued 1986, retired 1990. All bears measure 2-1/2 – 3-1/2in (6 – 9cm), cast in porcelain bisque.

257

258

259

LEFT to RIGHT:

257.   **Top Row:** *Shepherd; 2 Sheep; Nativity Angel - Banjo; Drummer; Nativity Angel - Horn; Nativity Angel - Harp:* issued 1986, retired 1990, *Girl with Shopping Bag:* issued 1986, retired 1988. **Second Row:** *Boy with Presents:* issued 1986, retired 1988, *Santa with "Merry Christmas" Banner; Couple Singing Christmas Carols; Bear Sitting Reading Book; Bear Standing Reading Book:* issued 1986, retired 1987, *Father Christmas:* issued 1986, retired 1988. **Third Row:** *Father Christmas:* issued 1986, retired 1988, *"Our 1st Christmas Together 1986":* issued 1986, retired 1986, *2 Nativity Angels:* issued 1987, retired 1990; *2 Shepherds with Sheep; Bear Holding Toy Horse:* issued 1987, open edition. **Bottom Row:** *Clown Juggling "NOEL"; Bear in Nightgown; Girl in Nightie and Night Cap; Boy Holding Stocking; Girl Holding Stocking:* issued 1987, retired 1989, *Santa Holding Teddy Bear:* issued 1987, retired 1988, *Night Before Christmas Santa with Toys:* issued 1987, retired 1993, *Girl Holding Doll:* issued 1987, retired 1989. All bears measure 2 – 3-1/2in (5 – 9cm), cast in porcelain bisque.

258.   **Top Row:** *Boy with Train; Girl with Teddy Bear; Mom and Son with Cookies; Girl in Green Coat with Handbag; Boy Pulling Tree in Sled:* issued 1987, retired 1989, *Shoemaker:* issued 1987, retired 1988. **Second Row:** *Boy at Work Table; Boy with Present:* issued 1987, retired 1989, *Girl in Victorian Dress:* issued 1987, retired 1988, *Girl in Night Cap; Mom with Pie:* issued 1987, retired 1989. **Third Row:** *Girl with Present; Boy with Present:* issued 1987, retired 1989, *Boy Playing Drum:* issued 1987, retired 1987, *2 Bears Dressed as Reindeer:* issued 1987, retired 1990, *Papa Bear and Wood Stove:* issued 1987, retired 1993, *Bear Making Cranberry Garland:* issued 1987, retired 1989. **Bottom Row:** *1st through 7th Day of Christmas:* issued 1987, retired 1988. All bears measure 3 – 3-1/2in (8 – 9cm), cast in porcelain bisque.

259.   **Top Row:** *8th through 12th Day of Christmas; Boy Skier:* issued 1987, retired 1988. **Second Row:** *Girl and Boy Building a Snowman:* issued 1989, retired 1989, *Little Bear Making Snowballs:* issued 1988; retired 1990, *Clara from "Nutcracker Suite":* issued 1988, retired 1989, *"1988" Nutcracker:* issued 1988, retired 1988, *"Nutcracker Suite" Sugar Plum Fairy:* issued 1988, retired 1989. **Third Row:** *2 Choir Bears Singing; Couple Kissing Under the Mistletoe:* issued 1988, retired 1989, *Bear Dressed as a Snowman:* issued 1988, open edition, *Ballerina Fairy:* issued 1988, retired 1989, *Bear Dressed as Star:* issued 1988, retired 1990, *Skier in Yellow Outfit:* issued 1988, retired 1990. **Bottom Row:** *St. Lucia:* issued 1989, retired 1990, *Bear Dressed as a Christmas Tree:* issued 1989, open edition, *Gnome Skiing; Gnome Smoking Pipe; Nativity Bunny, Goose; Dove; Chicken:* issued 1989, retired 1990. All bears measure 2-1/2 – 3-1/2in (6 – 9cm), cast in porcelain bisque.

260

261

263

263

262

LEFT to RIGHT:

260.   **Top Row:** *"A Christmas Carol" Scrooge Dated 1989:* issued 1989, retired 1989, *3 Tumbling Gnomes:* issued 1990, open edition, *Bears Dressed as Ball Ornaments - Red, Green:* issued 1990, retired 1993. **Second Row:** *Bear Dressed as Ornament - Blue:* issued 1990, retired 1993, *"1990" Bear Dressed as Holly Wreath:* issued 1990, retired 1990, *Bear Holding Mistletoe; 2 Cross-Country Skiers; Elve Building Toys (1 of 6 Pieces):* issued 1990, open edition. **Third Row:** *2 Elves Building Toys (2 of 6 Pieces); Gnome Carrying Stack of Gifts; Bear Dressed as a Jingle Bell; Girl Skater; Boy Skater:* issued 1990, open edition. **Bottom Row:** *Girl/Boy Skier with Broken Leg:* issued 1990, open edition, *Bear Dressed as a Holly Bush with Dove; Bear Dressed as Pine Cone; Elf Holding Gingerbread Cookie:* issued 1991, open edition, *"1991" Bear Dressed as Peppermint Candy:* issued 1991, retired 1991. All bears measure 2-1/2 – 3in (6 – 8cm), cast in porcelain bisque.

261.   **Top Row:** *4 Marching Band Members:* issued 1982, retired 1986, *Boy Bear with Bunny Ears:* issued 1979, retired 1985. **Bottom Row:** *Nativity Bear on Camel:* issued 1989, retired 1990, *Bear on Rocking Horse:* issued 1981, retired 1986, *Bear Dressed as Witch:* issued 1984, retired 1988, *Girl Bear with Bunny Ears:* issued 1979, retired 1985. All bears measure 3 – 3-1/4in (8 – 8.65cm), cast in porcelain bisque.

262.   *Bear Dressed as Vase of Roses:* 2-3/4in (7cm), *Bear Dressed as Birthday Cake:* 3-1/2in (9cm), both issued 1995, open edition, cast in porcelain bisque.

263.   *Boy Square Dancer:* 3in (8cm), *Girl Square Dancer:* 2-3/4in (7cm), both issued 1995, open edition, cast in porcelain bisque.

264

265

267

268

266

269

270

264. **Statue of Liberty:** 2-3/4in (7cm), **Uncle Sam:** 3-1/4in (8.65cm), both issued 1995, open edition, cast in porcelain bisque.

265. **Bear Holding Report Card:** 2-1/4in (5.65cm), issued 1995, open edition, cast in porcelain bisque.

266. **Bear Dressed as Trophy:** 2-3/4in (7cm), issued 1995, open edition, cast in porcelain bisque.

267. **Bear Dressed as Bride:** 2-3/4in (7cm) issued 1995, open edition, cast in porcelain bisque.

268. **Bear Dressed as Ballerina:** 2-3/4in (7cm), issued 1995, open edition, cast in porcelain bisque.

269. **World Greatest Secretary:** 2-3/4in (7cm), **Kiss the Cook:** 3-1/4in (8.65cm), both issued 1995, open edition, cast in porcelain bisque.

270. **Fishing Creel:** issued 1994, open edition, 2-3/4in (7cm), cast in porcelain bisque.

271

272

273

274

275

276

271. **Bears Dressed as Vegetable Crates; Tomatoes, Cucumbers, Carrots, Lettuce:** issued 1993, open edition, all measure 2-3/4in (7cm) cast in porcelain bisque.

272. **Bluebird:** 2-3/4in (7cm), issued 1992, open edition, **Butterfly:** 2-1/2in (6cm), issued 1991, open edition, cast in porcelain bisque.

273. **Daffodil and Daisy in Pot:** issued 1992, open edition, both measure 3in (8cm), cast in porcelain bisque.

274. **Lily and Pansy:** issued 1991, open edition, both measure 3in (8cm), cast in porcelain bisque.

275. **Picnic Basket:** issued 1994, open edition, 2-1/2in (6cm), cast in porcelain bisque.

276. **Bear Holding Bingo Card:** 2-1/2in (6cm), issued 1995, open edition, cast in porcelain bisque.

277

278

LEFT to RIGHT:

277. Sweet Shop Favorites, *Eclair; Ice Cream; Cupcake; Pie-a-La-mode:* all issued 1994, open edition. *Ice Cream Sandwich:* issued 1994, *Banana Split:* issued 1993, *Strawberry Shortcake:* issued 1994, *Slice of Cake:* issued 1994. All measure 2-3/4in (7cm) to 3in (8cm), open edition, cast in porcelain bisque.

278. *Ice Cream Sundae:* 2-3/4in (7cm), *Ice Cream Soda:* 2-1/2in (6 cm), both issued 1992, open edition, cast in porcelain bisque.

279

280

281

282

283

284

279. **Lucy as Birth Certificate:** issued
1994, open edition, 2-1/2in (6cm),
cast in porcelain bisque.
280. **Carton of Milk:** 2-3/4in (7cm),
Chocolate Cookie: 2-1/2in (6cm),
Chocolate Candy: 2-3/4in (7cm),
all issued 1992, open edition, cast
in porcelain bisque.
281. **Mail Box:** 3in (8cm), **Envelope:**
2-1/4in (5.65cm), both issued 1994,
open edition, cast in porcelain
bisque.
282. **3 Baby Bottles:** issued 1994, open
edition, 3-1/4in (5.65cm), cast in
porcelain bisque.
283. **Doctor in Scrubs:** issued 1994,
2-1/2in (6cm), cast in porcelain
bisque.
284. **Bear Dressed as Birdhouse:**
3-1/2in (9cm), **Watering Can:**
2-3/4in (7cm), both issued 1994,
open edition, cast in porcelain
bisque.

285

286

287

288

290

289

291

285. ***Bear Dressed as Clam:*** issued 1991, open edition, ***Tropical Fish:*** issued 1992, open edition. ***Bear Dressed as Lobster:*** issued 1991, open edition, ***Bear Dressed as Dolphin:*** issued 1992, open edition. All bears measure 2-1/2 – 3in (6 – 8cm), cast in porcelain bisque.

286. ***Jar of Baby Food; Ring Toy:*** issued 1994, both measure 3in (8cm), cast in porcelain bisque.

287. ***Tyrannosaurus Dinosaur; Stegosauraus Dinosaur; Tricerotops Dinosaur:*** issued 1992, open edition. All measure 2-3/4 – 3in (7 – 8cm), cast in porcelain bisque.

288. ***Groucho:*** 2-1/2in (6cm), ***Harpo:*** 2-3/4in (7cm), both issued 1992, open edition, cast porcelain bisque.

289. Bible Classic - ***Eve:*** 2-3/4in (7cm). ***Adam:*** 2-1/2in (6cm), both issued 1992, open edition, cast in porcelain bisque.

290. ***Lucy as an Animal Lover:*** issued 1991, open edition, 2-3/4in (7cm), cast in porcelain bisque.

291. ***Beautician:*** issued 1994, 3in (8cm), cast in porcelain bisque.

292. ***Phantom of the Opera:*** issued 1991, open edition, 2-3/4in (7cm), cast in porcelain bisque.

292

293

295

294

296

297

293. *Construction Worker:* 2-1/2in (6cm), *Teacher:*
2-1/2in (6 cm), *Policeman:* 3in (8cm), issued 1994,
open edition, cast in porcelain bisque.

294. *Birthday Parade*, Age 5; *Birthday Parade*, Age 6.
Birthday Parade 2; Birthday Parade, Age 3;
Birthday Parade, Age 4. *Birthday Parade*, Age 1.
All issued 1992, open edition, all pieces measure
2-1/2 – 3in (6 – 8cm), cast in porcelain bisque.

295. *Bear Holding Toothbrush:* 2-1/2in (6cm), *Bear
Dressed as Toothpaste:* 3in (8cm), issued 1992,
open edition, cast in porcelain bisque.

296. *Loving Cup 15th Anniversary Piece:* limited to year
of issue (1993), 2- 1/2in (6cm), cast in
porcelain bisque.

297. *Lucy and Me Collector's Sign:* issued 1991,
open edition, 2-1/2in (6cm), cast in porcelain bisque.

298

299

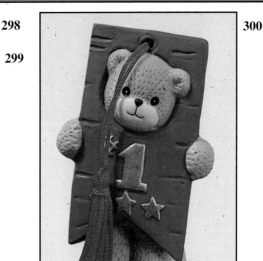

300

301

303

302

304

305

298. *Lucy and Me Limited Edition:* issued 1995, Limited Edition of 2000, 3in (8cm), cast in porcelain bisque.

299. *Bear Holding 1st Place Ribbon:* issued 1995, open edition, 2-3/4in (7cm), cast in porcelain bisque.

300. *Bear Dressed as Dice:* issued 1995, open edition, 2-3/4in (7cm), cast in porcelain bisque.

301. *Baby in Christening Gown:* issued 1992, open edition, 2-1/4in (5.65cm), cast in porcelain bisque.

302. *Nurse:* 2-3/4in (7cm), *Hot Water Bottle:* 3in (8cm), issued 1992, open edition, cast in porcelain bisque.

303. *Owl:* 3in (8cm), *Noah's Ark Kangaroo:* 3in (8cm), *Frog:* 2-1/4in (5.65cm), all issued 1991, retired 1993, cast in porcelain bisque.

304. *Three Crayons: Yellow, Red, Blue:* issued 1991, retired 1993, all measure 3-1/4in (8.65cm), cast in porcelain bisque.

305. *Pizza:* issued 1991, open edition, 3-1/4in (8.65cm), cast in porcelain bisque.

306

307

308

309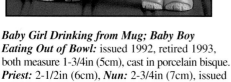

310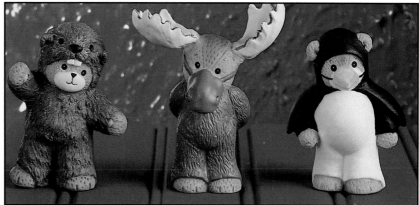

311

312

313

306. ***Baby Girl Drinking from Mug; Baby Boy Eating Out of Bowl:*** issued 1992, retired 1993, both measure 1-3/4in (5cm), cast in porcelain bisque.

307. ***Priest:*** 2-1/2in (6cm), ***Nun:*** 2-3/4in (7cm), issued 1992, open edition, cast in porcelain bisque.

308. ***Lone Ranger; Tonto:*** issued 1991, open edition, 2-3/4in (7cm), cast in porcelain bisque.

309. ***Bear Dressed as Kite:*** 3-1/4in (8.65cm), ***Bear Dressed as Rainbow/Sun:*** 2-3/4in (7cm), issued 1991, retired 1993, cast in porcelain bisque.

310. ***Beaver:*** 2-1/2in (6cm), ***Moose:*** 3-1/4in (8.65cm), ***Penguin:*** 2-1/2in (6cm), all issued 1992, open edition, cast in porcelain bisque.

311. ***"Take a Hike", the Walker:*** issued 1992, open edition, 2-1/2in (6cm), cast in porcelain bisque.

312. ***Snail; Caterpillar:*** issued 1991, open edition, 3in (8cm), cast in porcelain bisque.

313. ***Bear Dressed as Bowling Pin:*** issued 1991, open edition, 4in (10cm), cast in porcelain bisque.

314

315

316

314. ***Raspberry, Cherry, Blueberry, Strawberry:*** issued
      1992, open edition, 2-3/4in (7cm), cast in
      porcelain bisque.
315. ***Gingerbread House:*** 6in (15cm), ceramic, ***Hansel
      and Gretel:*** 2-3/4in (7cm), issued 1991, retired
      1993, cast in porcelain bisque.
316. ***Navy; Marine; Army; Air Force:*** all issued 1991,
      retired 1993, all measure 2-3/4 in (7cm), cast in
      porcelain bisque.

317

318

319

320

317. *Nathan; Shawnie:* issued 1995, 5in (13cm), nominated for 1995 TOBY® Award, cast in porcelain bisque, limited edition 2000, open edition.

318. *Beth; Thomas:* issued 1995, 5in (13cm), cast in porcelain bisque, limited edition 2000 each, open edition.

319. *Mrs. Claus; Santa Claus:* issued 1995, 5in (13cm), cast in porcelain bisque, limited edition 2000 each, open edition.

320. *Frances; Mary Louise:* issued 1995, 5in (13cm), cast in porcelain bisque, limited edition 2000 each, open edition.

321

322

323

324

325

321. *Rachel; Angela:* issued 1995, 3in (8cm), cast in porcelain bisque, limited edition 5000 each, open edition.

322. *Amy:* issued 1995, 3in (8cm), cast in porcelain bisque, limited edition 5000, open edition.

323. *Debra; Muriel:* issued 1995, 3in (8cm), cast in porcelain bisque, limited edition 5000 each, open edition.

324. *Carrie:* issued 1995, 3in (8cm), cast in porcelain bisque, limited edition 5000, open edition.

325. *Susie; Allison:* issued 1994, 5in (13cm), cast in porcelain bisque, limited edition 2000 each, open edition.

326

Diane

Joan

327

Romeo

Juliet

328

Denise
Spring

329

330

Carol
Winter

331

Emily
Summer

326. *"Diane", the Bride; "Joan", with Hand Mirror; "Linda", with Tea Cup:* issued 1994, 6-1/2in (16cm), cast in porcelain bisque, limited edition 2000 each, closed edition.

327. *Juliet; Romeo:* issued 1994, 5in (13cm), cast in porcelain bisque, limited edition 2000 each, open edition.

328. *"Denise", Spring:* issue 1995, 5in (13cm), cast in porcelain bisque, limited edition 2000, open edition.

329. *"Melissa", Autumn:* issued 1995, 5in (13cm), cast in porcelain bisque, limited edition 2000, open edition.

330. *"Carol", Winter:* issued 1995, 5in (13cm), cast in porcelain bisque, limited edition 2000, open edition.

331. *"Emily", Summer:* issued 1995, 5in (13cm), cast in porcelain bisque, limited edition 20000, open edition.

In 1994, the PennyWhistle Collection, a charming minature collection of antique toys, teddies, and dolls, was introduced by Enesco. Each piece is sculpted to detail from Peter Fagan's personal collection located at his home number one PennyWhistle Lane. Peter is an enthusiastic collector! His home is overflowing with antique and victorian teddy bears, toys, miniatures and memorabilia that the artist has gathered from the far corners of the

world. Peter shares his affection for these pieces with collectors by modeling perfect miniatures of those closest to his heart. Each piece is cast in porcelain and hand painted. A captivating story detailing the unique history of the piece accompanies each one.

Enesco® has plans to add new pieces to the collection. These miniatures are sure to capture the hearts of collectors worldwide.

332

333

335

336

334

337

338

332. *Letter To Santa:* issued 1995, 5in (13cm), cold-cast porcelain, open edition.

333. *Trunk of Teddies:* issued 1995, 4in (10cm), cold-cast porcelain, limited edition 1000.

334. *Jingles Better Bear:* issued 1995, 2in (5cm), cold-cast porcelain, open edition.

335. *Priscilla:* issued 1995, 1-3/4in (5cm), cold-cast porcelain, open edition.

336. *George:* issued 1994, 2in (5cm), cold-cast porcelain, open edition.

337. *Ben; Davey:* issued 1994, 1in (3cm), cold-cast porcelain, open edition.

338. *Prudence:* issued 1994, 2in (5cm), cold-cast porcelain, open edition.

The Centimental Bears is another collection by Scottish artist Peter Fagan. This collection represents the best-loved European Bears. "Cousins" to the bears inhabiting Number One PennyWhistle Lane, each figurine has its own story and comes with a teddy bear "coin" representing love and friendship. Each figurine is cast in porcelain and hand painted. The Centimental Bears are divided into four groups: Love and Friendship, Spring, Halloween, and Winter/Christmas. Each bear in this collection varies in size and color, making the collection more appealing to collectors.

Peter Fagan again has captured the characteristics of friendship that all Teddies seem to share.

339

339. **Centimental Bears Halloween Collection:
Left to Right:** *Meekie's Lantern; Wizard
Litmus; Reggie, the Halloween Bandit;
Sopwith Gets Ready; Nym's Black Cat;
Binkies' Pumpkin; Spooky Ralph; Irvine's
Trick or Treat:* issued 1995, figurines
measure 1 – 2in (3 – 5cm), cast in
porcelain, open edition.
340. ***Christopher and Gustav:*** issued 1995,
1-3/4in (5cm), cast in porcelain, open edition.
341. ***Regina:*** 2-1/4in (5.65cm), ***Ian:*** 1-3/4in (5cm),
issued 1995, cast in porcelain, open edition.
342. ***Kenny:*** issued 1995, 2-3/4in (5cm), cast in
porcelain, open edition.

340

341

342

343

344

About The Artist:
PETER FAGAN

Deep in the beautiful hills of the Scottish Borders, artist Peter Fagan established his design studios. The gentle scenery and the traditional history of crafts in this part of Scotland provide Peter with a creative working atmosphere. However, he is not just a talented and imaginative artist, he is a collector -- of antiques, toys and teddy bears.

His home is filled with an array of antiques and memorabilia, collections of Victorian miniatures and ancient teddy bears and toys. Peter shares his collections with others by modeling perfect miniatures of some characters and objects that are close to his heart. His work is a family collaboration, since every piece in his own collection has a story written by his wife, Frances.

Peter began his career sculpting miniature cold cast bronze figurines and locally selling them. He later changed the medium of his sculptures to resin and hand painted them. In 1973, he established a company called Bronze Age Ltd. from his home and named the new collection of collectibles Colour Box.

Today Colour Box is one of Britain's major giftware companies, which produces over 300 sculptures in five main collectible ranges. The collection most recognized in the United States is PennyWhistle Lane. This Collection of colorful resin figurines has taken the U.S. miniature market by storm and currently rates among the top ten miniature collections.

Peter is an artist with a vision who is backed by his wife Frances, the storyteller and marketing manager. All of his collections are known for their wealth of detail and quality, characteristics that make his work world renowned. The Fagans currently reside in Lauder, Scotland with their four children.

345

346

347

343. ***Squidge; Mr. Perkins; Vernon; Red Bear:*** issued 1995, bears measure 1 – 2in (3 – 5cm), cast in porcelain, open edition.

344. ***Cousin Eccy:*** 1-1/2in (4cm), ***Bruno:*** 3in (8cm), ***Emlyn:*** 3in (8cm), issued 1995, cast in porcelain, open edition.

345. ***Peter Bear:*** 2in (5cm), ***Timmy:*** 2-3/4in (7cm), ***Arabella:*** 2-3/4in (7cm), ***Elly May:*** 2-1/4in (5.65cm), issued 1995, cast in porcelain, open edition.

346. ***Baron Von Berne:*** 3in (8cm), ***Sullivan:*** 3in (8cm), ***Ollie:*** 3in (8cm), issued 1995, cast in porcelain, open edition.

347. Centimental Bears Spring Collection; ***Morris Minor:*** 2in (5cm), ***Joseph:*** 1-3/4in (5cm), ***Bernard:*** 2-3/4in (7cm), ***Teddy Robinson:*** 1in (3cm), ***Chocolate Chip:*** 1-3/4in (5 cm), all issued 1995, cast in porcelain, open edition.

FORT®, INC.

Fort®, Inc., a company known for fine pewter gift-ware was founded in 1945. In 1993, Jim Forte, president of Fort®, Inc., thought about issuing a special holiday piece. He decided it should incorporate the word joy, with the "J" standing for Jesus, the "O" for others and "Y" for yourself. As the idea developed, a teddy bear was added to each letter, and the three pieces, designed by artist-in-residence Shawn Slother, were given the name "Joy Bears." Due to the overwhelming response to Joy Bears™, Fort®, Inc. decided to create an entire collection of miniature pewter teddies.

The Joy Bears™ Collection was introduced in stores January 1994 with 30 pieces; 22 miniature teddy bear figurines and 8 accessory pieces. The collection was sculpted by in-house artist Shawn Slother, a artist known for his intricate detail. Each

piece in the collection is modeled after an original Then Slother creates his sculptures by the "additive process". Using a hard wax, which becomes pliable as it warms up, he builds the pieces and adds realistic details. Even with their small size, Slother is able to add amazing detail to each piece in the collection. For example, if you look at the "Joyous Snooze", you'll see that you can read the name of the newspaper that has slipped down onto Grandpa Bear's lap. Even accessories, such as the couch, have great detail.

In addition to being finely detailed, the pieces in the collection have been designed with collectors in mind. The figurines range in size from 1-1/2 to 2-1/2 inches high, and retail at $15 to $40 each, with most under $25. The accessory pieces range between $20 and $50 each. Fort®, Inc., has future plans to add to the Joy Bears™ Collection.

348

349

350

351

352

353

348. **Sis:** issued 1994, 2-1/2in (6cm), cast in pewter, open edition.

349. **Topper:** issued 1994, 2-1/2in (6cm), cast in pewter, open edition.

350. **Cubby:** issued 1994, 2-1/4in (5.65cm), cast in pewter, open edition.

351. **Reach for the Stars:** issued 1994, 1993 nomination for Miniature of the Year, 3in (8cm), cast in pewter, open edition.

352. **Bundled Up:** issued 1994, 2-1/2in (6cm), cast in pewter, open edition.

353. **Do-Re-Mi:** issued 1994, 1-3/4in (5cm), cast in pewter, open edition.

354

About The Artist: SHAWN SLOTHER

Artist Shawn Slother was born and raised in Titusville, Pennsylvania. Slother enjoyed painting and sculpting during his teen years, but it was an appreticeship with the late master sculptor John Imhoff, who lived in his hometown, that inspired him to pursue a career as an artist. Slother attended Edinboro University, a division of the University Pennsylvania system, where he earned a Bachelor of Fine Arts degree in 1992. After graduation, Slother joined Fort's artist-in residence program, where he has created a number of the company's Disney® and sports pieces, including the Golf Chess Set, which received a nomination for a 1993 Collector's Edition Award of Excellence.

Though Slother did not have teddy bears in his childhood, he has had an affinity for them since his wife, Sonja, collects them. On their first date, which was Sonja's birthday, Slother gave her a teddy bear. Today Slother gives a different teddy bear to his wife on her birthday. His wife has about 30 to 40 plush bears. Slother gets his inspiration for the Joy Bears™ from his wife's teddy bear collection and his own childhood memories.

Slother has received a two-time nomination from *Collector's Edition* Magazine in two categories. In 1993, the Joy Bear™ figurine "Reach for the Stars" was nominated for Miniature of the Year. This was especially nice because Fort®, Inc., had pledged a percentage of the profits from "Reach for the Stars" to the Starlight Foundation, a charity that helps seriously ill children and their families. Slother feels the Joy Bears™ represent life's little joys and those fleeting moments that become our fondest memories.

355

356

359

357

358

360

361

362

354.   **Mr. Snowbear:** issued 1994, 2-1/2in (6cm), cast in pewter, open edition.

355.   **Flyin':** issued 1994, 2-1/2in (6cm), cast in pewter, open edition.

356.   **Rollie:** issued 1994, 1-3/4in (5cm), cast in pewter, open edition.

357.   **Joyous Snooze:** issued 1994, 1-3/4in (5cm) cast in pewter, open edition.

358.   **Joyful Surprise:** issued 1994, 1-1/2in (4cm), cast in pewter, open edition.

359.   **Ooops:** issued 1994, 2-1/4in (5.65cm), cast in pewter, open edition.

360.   **Open Arms:** issued 1994, 2-1/2in (6cm), cast in pewter, open edition.

361.   **Just Checkin':** issued 1994, 1-3/4 x 1-1/2in (5 x 4cm), cast in pewter, open edition.

362.   **Cooky:** issued 1994, 2-1/2in (6cm), cast in pewter, open edition.

Kit Cropper created five of the six porcelain and mixed media figurines for the Historical House of Bears; the sixth is a licensed figure of Smokey Bear® sculpted by Linda Grucza. Like the stuffed teddies, the figurines represent the various eras of original Knickerbocker bears, ranging from 1933 to the 1960s. The collection is available until 1997. Knickerbocker has plans to introduce other figures in the coming year.

393

394

395

396

398

397

393.   *75th Anniversary House of Bears;* **Clockwise from Top Right:** *Papa, Mama, Brother, Sister, Mimmi and Smokey Bear®.* Display House measures 10-1/2 x 16in (26 x 41cm).

394.   *Papa Bear:* issued 1995, 4-1/2in (11cm), cast in resin, open edition. Papa is from the post-World War II period when Knickerbocker traditional designs were typified by the inset, rounded muzzle of clipped plush. During this era Knickerbocker Bears had a rounder head, high forehead, wide set eyes and a chubby body.

395.   *Mama Bear:* issued 1995, 4in (10cm), cast in resin, open edition. Mama, like Papa, is also from the post-World War II period.

396.   *Brother Bear:* issued 1995, 2-1/2in (6cm), cast in resin, open edition. Brother is reminiscent of the 1950's "Joy of a Toy" collection. He has a rounded head, chubby body and "bat" ears - so called because of their large, flat, "C" shaped design.

397.   *Sister Bear:* issued 1995, 3in (8cm), cast in resin, open edition. Sister bear is from the cuddly era of the 1940's. She has been sculpted in a rich golden shade and has the rounded head, wide set eyes and chubby limbs the Knickerbocker post war bears were known for.

398.   *Smokey Bear®:* issued 1995, 4-3/4in (12cm), cast in resin, open edition. Smokey was originally produced by Knickerbocker from the 1960's through 1977. He has been created to the exact specifications of the USDA Forest Service.

399

399.   *Mimmi Bear:* issued 1995, 3in (8cm), cast in resin, open edition. Mimmi represents the Knickerbocker grandmother bear. Fashioned after a 1933 Cinnamon bear, this bear has the traditional pointed muzzle design of the pre-World War II bears.

NEVENSCHWANDER ARTWORKS

BREAD N' BUTTER BEARS

Robert and Lesli Nevenschwander operate as a husband and wife team. Nevenschwander Artwork began in 1986 under the name of Nevenswander Wooden Dolls. The original "Bread N' Butter Bears" was introduced the following year. The collection of bears was based upon original cartoons by Lesli Nevenschwander which were translated into wooden form by Robert Nevenschwander. Robert Nevenschwander is a master carver who continues creating one-of-a-kind artist dolls but finds the bears to be fun and a means of escape. Together Robert and Lesli has created a line of unique bear

characters. They have plans to introduce new pieces to the collection. The company has started a collector's club for the Bread N' Butter Bears, a club that introduces the collector to new figurines and a exclusive club figurine, the "Logo Bear". Robert Nevenschwander has written a book on carving comical cartoon bears published by Schiffer Publishing. This book is filled with step by step instructions on carving wooden bears.

Bread N' Butter Bears are sure to be popular to teddy figurine collectors. These figurines are unique in style and will bring many hours of collecting joy.

400

401

402

403

404

400. **Bread N' Butter Bears:** first introduced 1988, figurines measure 3-3/4 – 4-3/4in (10 – 12cm), hand-carved wood-resin, open edition. Photo courtesy Schiffer Publishing.

401. **Lori, Hope, Sabrina, Mimi;** jointed dolls, handcarved from Linden wood, mohair wig, issued 1995, limited edition, 8 pieces, 9 1/2 inches (23.1 cm).

402. **Lenita:** one-of-kind, handcarved from Linden wood, mohair wig, silk dress, issued 1994; 19-1/2in (49cm).

403. **Logo Bear:** Bread N' Butter Bear's collector club figurine, issued 1994, handcarved wood-resin, 2-1/4in (5.65cm), open edition.

404. **Abearham Lincoln:** issued 1995, hand-carved wood-resin bear, 5-3/4in (15cm), open edition.

NORTH AMERICAN BEAR CO., INC.

MUFFY VANDERBEAR COLLECTION

In the mid 1970's, while raising a small child and studying ceramic and toy design, Barbara Isenberg decided to start a toy company to produce uniquely designed, high quality teddy bears. The bears would have the nostalgic charm of antique toys, with an appeal for both children and adults. She asked her fashion designer friend, Old Bauer, to make a bear out of an old sweatshirt that would be soft, cuddly and different from anything else on the market. That bear evolved into Albert the Running Bear, a classic bear in a colorful running suit.

In 1978, after perfecting a variety of sample bears and finding a sales force and a small New York City factory to produce the bears, Barbara teamed up with her brother, Paul Levy, to form the North American Bear Co., Inc. A year after Albert the Running Bear was produced, the VIB line (dressed velour bears with pun names) was introduced on the market. These were followed by the VanderBear Family in 1983 and Muffy VanderBear in 1984. The North American Bear Co. has now diversified into a full range of other plush toys, each having it's own look and name. It has also expanded into accessories, greetings, paper products and a full line of infant plush. Their distribution is global and foreign sales are growing.

North American Bear Company introduced a color flock over plastic figurines in 1989, these were Mini V.I.B.'s. There were eight in the collection. Each individually boxed piece stood 4inches high. In 1990 three other pieces: Anna Bearvlova, Amelia Bearhart, and William Shakesbear were introduced. All pieces were retired in the fall of 1992.

At the Fall 1992 Walt Disney World® Teddy Bear Convention, the company introduced three storybook Mini V.I.B.'s. All 4 inch figurines were individually box and available only at this convention.

In 1994 North American introduced Muffy VanderBear Figurine Collection. Each of the five 3 inch poly-resin figurines is individually box. This is currently the only collection North America Bear Company has in production. The company has no future plans to introduce any other figurine collections.

405

406

407

405. *V.I.B. Collection,* **Top Left:** *Mitzber; Bearilyn Monroe; Humphrey Beargart I; Laura Beareall; Clara Bearton.* **Bottom Left:** *Bear Ruth; Rhett Beartler; Scarlett O'Beara II; Dr. Kilbear:* 4in (10cm), issued 1989; color-flocking covered over molded plastic, retired 1992.

406. **Left to Right:** *Alice in Wonbearland; Snow Bear and the Seven Cubs, Cinbearella:* 4in (10cm), issued 1992, molded after limited edition V.I.B.s that were created exclusively for the Annual Walt Disney World® Teddy Bear Convention; colored flocking over molded plastic, retired 1992.

407. *Muffy VanderBear™ Collection,* **Left to Right:** *Muffy Day in the County; Muffy Safari; Muffy High Tea; Muffy Sailor; Muffy Gibearny:* 3in (8cm), issued 1994, cast in resin, open edition.

109

PACIFIC RIM IMPORT CORPORATION

408

PUDDLEBROOK® TEDDIES

Pacific Rim Import is a national importer and distributor based in Seattle, Washington. The company has been in business for over 40 years. Pacific Rim is the producer of many product lines including seasonal decoratives, silk flowers, and a large collection of home and garden accessories.

In 1990, Pacific Rim, introduced its first collectible product line of porcelain Village Bristol Township and Waterfront by artist Pat Sebern. Then in 1994, the company introduced its first resin figurine collection called Bunny Toes, a series of small resin bunnies. In 1995, the first teddy bear figurine collection, the Puddlebrook® Teddies by artist Pat Sebern, was introduced.

The collection of resin teddy figurines measure 3-1/2 inches. Each figurine is dressed in victorian winter clothes. The teddies are the first of a Christmas series of four bears shown tumbling around on the ice and snow.

Pat Sebern is working on new Puddlebrook® figurines which will be introduced in late 1996. The Puddlebrook® Teddies are sure to be a popular collectible.

408. **Top to Bottom; Left to Right:** *Collecting the Tree; Ice Dancers; Taking a Tumble; Sledding Fun:* issued 1995, 3-1/2in (9cm), cast in resin.

PENNI JO ORIGINALS

PENNIBEARS™ COLLECTION

A few years ago, Penni Jo Jonas was a homemaker who had no idea she would have such a successful artistic career. The phenomenon of her teddy bear creations has propelled her into the national spotlight.

Penni Jo's first creations were made in her kitchen, using colored clays she mixed in her food processor and baked in her toaster oven. A miniature teddy bear she made for her daughter's doll house became the inspiration for a series of similar bears. These little bears were sculpted with clothes and accessories and eventually became known as PenniBears™. The PenniBears™ are sculpted with outstanding attention to detail. These figurine teddies have characteristic charm and personality.

PenniBears™ are 1-1/2 inch limited edition collectible miniatures hand-cast in bonded porcelain. Using Penni Jo's sculpted original, delicate molds capturing tiny detail are made. Cold casting in bonded porcelain allows the detail to ream in each cast piece, which is then carefully hand painted. A final protective coat of clear resin is applied and each PenniBear™ has a trademark copper penny inserted in its base. The mod marks identify the year

a PenniBear™ was produced. The mod mark for the first year of production is a heart; for the second year a bow; and for the third year, a flower. This remains consistent with each edition, with the exception of the first and second year's release of PB-001 through PB-052, on which there are no mold marks. PenniBears™ are limited to no more than three years production. The molds are then destroyed.

Penni Jo's PenniBears™ blossomed into a national following, and in 1989 Penni Jo joined the staff of United Design® where all the intricate details of PenniBears™ were reproduced by talented production artists and craftsmen. For nearly five years, PenniBears™ were manufactured and distributed by United Design® Corporation. In 1994, the PenniBears™ returned to Penni Jo's company, based in Moore, Oklahoma. The company manufacturing and distribution is being done by husband, Don Jonas, and the family, neighbors and friends of master sculptor, Penni Jo Jonas. These figurines are still being carefully handcrafted in true American cottage industry.

Collectors can register any PenniBear™ by having a collector's center send a registration card to Penni Jo's Originals.

Each PenniBear™ comes in a beautifully printed box, which includes a certificate of authenticity. Collectors should keep both the box and the certificate as valuable parts of their collection.

In addition, to Penni Jo's successful PenniBears™, Penni Jo designs and sculpts several other collectible figurine editions. Her new collection of Teddy Angels™ which is produced by United Design® Corporation is sure to be another successful teddy bear figurine collection.

Penni Jo is delightfully open and candid about her transition from homemaker to nationally renowned artist. Penni Jo loves to meet collectors and fans as much as they love her and the exquisite detail she is able to capture in her teddy bear figurines.

409

410

411

412

413

409. **Bear Capade:** issued 1992, 1-1/2in (4cm), cast in bonded porcelain, retired 1994.

410. **Left to Right: Bouquet Girl; Honey Bear; Bouquet Boy; Beautiful Bride:** issued 1989, 1/2 – 1-1/2in (1 – 4cm), cast in bonded porcelain, retired 1992.

411. **Left to Right: Butterfly Bear; Cookie Bandit; Baby Hugs** (1st in Bear babies); **Doctor Bear:** issued 1989, 1 – 1-1/2in (3 – 4cm), cast in bonded porcelain, retired 1992.

412. **Left to Right: Lazy Days; Petite Mademoiselle; Giddyup Teddy; Buttons and Bows:** issued 1989, 1/2 – 1-1/2in (1– 4cm), cast in bonded porcelain, retired 1992.

413. **Left to Right: Country Spring; Garden Path:** issued 1990, **Handsome Groom; Nap Time:** issued 1989, 1/2 – 1-1/2in (1 – 4cm), cast in bonded porcelain, retired 1992.

414

415

416

417

418

419

420

421

414. **Left to Right:** *Bearly Awake; Lil' Merteddy* (1st in stories and rhymes); *Bump-Bear Crop* (and in Founding folks); *Country Lullaby; Bear Footin's It:* issued 1991, 1in (3cm), cast in bonded porcelain, retired 1993.

415. *On Your Toes:* issued 1992, 1-1/2in (4cm), cast in bonded porcelain, retired 1994.

416. **Left to Right:** *Windy Day; Bountiful Harvest; Christmas ReinBear; Pilgrim Provider* (3rd in Founding Folks); *Sweet Lil' Sis:* issued 1991, 1-1/2in (4cm), cast in bonded porcelain, retired 1994.

417. *Left to Right: Boooo Bear; Sneaky Snowball* (1st in winter fun); *Count Bearacula; Dress Up Fun:* issued 1990, 1-1/2in (4cm), cast in bonded porcelain, retired 1993.

418. **PenniBear™ Collector's Club Members Only Editions:** *Chalk Up Another Year:* issued 1993, 1in (3cm), cast in bonded porcelain, retired.

419. **Left to Right:** *Scarecrow Teddy; Country Quilt* (1st in Founding Folks); *Santa Bear-ing Gifts; Stocking Surprise:* issued 1990, 1 – 1-1/2in (3 – 4cm), cast in bonded porcelain, retired 1993.

420. **Left to Right:** *Nurse Bear* (1st nurse bear); *Birthday Bear* (1st Party-time series); *Attic Fun; Puppy Bath:* issued 1989, 1 – 1-1/2in (1 – 4cm), cast in bonded porcelain, retired 1992.

421. **Left to Right:** *Puppy Love; Tubby Teddy; Bathtime Buddies; Southern Belle:* issued 1989, 1 – 1-1/2in (3 – 4cm), cast in bonded porcelain, retired 1992.

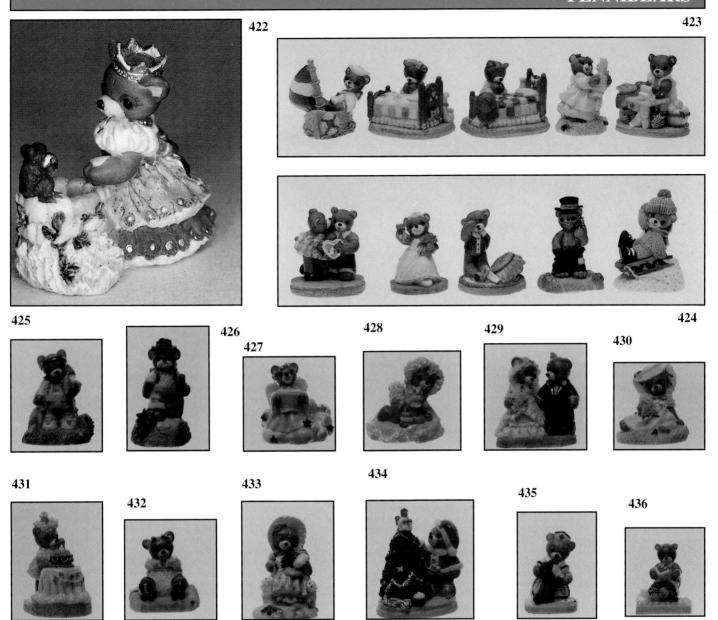

422

423

425

426

427

428

429

430

424

431

432

433

434

435

436

422.   *The Frog Princess:* issued 1995, 1in (3cm), cast in bonded porcelain, open edition.
423.   **Left to Right:** *Summer Sailing; Goodnight Sweet Princess; Goodnight Little Prince; Bunny Buddies; Baking Goodies:* issued 1991, 1-1/2in (4cm), cast in bonded porcelain, retired 1993.
424.   **Left to Right:** *Sweetheart Bears* (1st in Sweetheart Series); *Curtain Call; BooHoo Bear; Happy Hobo; A Wild Ride* (and in Winter Fun): issued 1991, 1-1/2in (4cm), cast in bonded porcelain, retired 1994.
425.   *Big Chief Little Bear:* issued 1993, 1 – 1-1/2in (3 – 4cm), cast in bonded porcelain, retired 1995.
426.   *A Happy Camper:* issued 1993, 1 – 1-1/2in (3 – 4cm), cast in bonded porcelain, retired 1995.
427.   *May Joy Be Yours:* issued 1993, 1 – 1-1/2in (3 – 4cm), cast in bonded porcelain, retired 1995.
428.   *Getting 'Round on My Own:* issued 1993, 1 – 1-1/2in (3 – 4cm), cast in bonded porcelain, retired 1995.
429.   *My Forever Love:* issued 1993, 1in (3cm), cast in bonded porcelain, retired 1995.
430.   *Summer Belle:* issued 1993, 1in (3cm), cast in bonded porcelain, retired 1995.
431.   *Happy Birthday:* issued 1993, 1in (3cm), cast in bonded porcelain, retired 1995.
432.   *Gotta Try Again:* issued 1993, 1in (3cm), cast in bonded porcelain, retired 1995.
433.   *Little Bear Peep:* issued 1993, 1 – 1-1/2in (3 – 4cm), cast in bonded porcelain, retired 1995.
434.   *Santa's Helpers:* issued 1993, 1 – 1-1/2in (3 – 4cm), cast in bonded porcelain, retired 1995.
435.   *Making It Better:* issued 1993, 1 – 1-1/2in (3 – 4cm), cast in bonded porcelain, retired 1995.
436.   *Rest Stop:* issued 1993, 1 – 1-1/2in (3 – 4cm), cast in bonded porcelain, retired 1995.

437

438

439

440

441

442

443

444

445

446

437. *Tally Ho; Sand Box Fun:* issued 1992, 1/2 – 1-1/2in (1 – 4cm), cast in bonded porcelain, retired 1994.

438. *Winter Friends:* issued 1994, 1-1/2in (4cm), cast in bonded porcelain, open edition.

439. *Saint-AHH:* issued 1994, 1-1/2in (4cm), cast in bonded porcelain, open edition.

440. *Two by Two:* issued 1994, 1in (3cm), cast in bonded porcelain, open edition.

441. *Victorian Foundations:* issued 1995, 1-1/2in (4cm), cast in bonded porcelain, open edition.

442. *Spanish Rose; "I Made It" Boy:* issued 1992, 1-1/2in (4cm), cast in bonded porcelain, retired 1994.

443. *Batter Up:* issued 1992, 1-1/2in (4cm), cast in bonded porcelain, retired 1994.

444. *Pot o' Gold; Down Hill Thrill:* issued 1992, 1-1/2in (4cm), cast in bonded porcelain, retired 1994.

445. *Dust Bunny Roundup:* issued 1992, 1-1/2in (4cm), cast in bonded porcelain, retired 1994.

446. *Touchdown, First Prom:* issued 1992, 1 – 1-1/2in (3 – 4cm), cast in bonded porcelain, retired 1994.

448

447

449

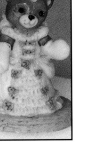

450

452

451

453

447. *Lil' Sis Makes Up; Puddle Jumper:* issued 1992, 1-1/2in (4cm), cast in bonded porcelain, retired 1994.

448. *Clowning Around; Decorating – the Wreath:* issued 1992, 1/2 – 1-1/2in (1 – 4cm), cast in bonded porcelain, retired 1994.

449. *"I Made It" Girl; Cinderella:* issued 1992, 1-1/2in (4cm), cast in bonded porcelain, retired 1994.

450. *Will You Be Mine; Smokey's Nephew:* issued 1992, 1in (3cm), cast in bonded porcelain, retired 1994.

451. **PenniBear™ Collector's Club Members Only Editions: Left to Right:** *First Collection* issued 1991, *Collecting Makes Cents* issued 1992, *Today's Pleasures, Tomorrow's Treasures* issued 1992, 1-1/2in (4cm), cast in bonded porcelain, retired.

452. A copper penny is cast in the bottom of each **PenniBear™** figurine.

453. *Apple for Teacher:* issued 1992, 1-1/2in (4cm), cast in bonded porcelain, retired 1994.

RAVENWOOD COLLECTION

In 1995 Raikes Originals introduced a handcarved wooden figurine line called Ravenwood by Robert Raikes. The pieces represent the first in a line of posable figurine characters that are part of the Ravenwood fantasy. Ravenwood is a land full of adventure, fun, and wonder, sprinkled with a touch of danger to challenge the virtue in the hearts of the good characters of Ravenwood. The Raikes goal is to create a fantasy in the tradition of *Grimms Fairy Tales, The Hobbit,* and C. S. Lewis' Chronicles of Narnia.

Work on the Ravenwood line began over 2-1/2 years ago. During that time, pieces of Ravenwood have been displayed at the Robert Raikes Collector's Club Conventions, as well as a number of stores and collector's shows, to judge the public's response to this new line. The pieces have been received with smiles and excitement. Only a few handmade original pieces have been available to collectors.

Currently, there are three of the all wood, jointed bears called Woodykins in production. The goal is to have them available for distribution by October-November 1995. Ravenwood production runs will be in editions of 250/500/1500/2000; with Artist's Proofs of 50 taken from each run. The size of the run will be determined by the character's subject matter and by the discretion of the sculptor, Robert Raikes. The price range will vary depending on the character and the accessories. The Woodykins should retail between $60 and $75; with some of the elf gnomes, fairies, and other characters retailing in prices from $115 and up. Artist's Proofs of each character with a special medallion and hand-signed by Raikes will be slightly more expensive.

Collectors will soon be meeting the various characters of Ravenwood.

454

455

456

About the Artist:
ROBERT RAIKES

Robert Raikes has been a sculptor for over 25 years. During his career, he has created hundreds of sculptures including human figures, animals, fantasy pieces, art dolls, carousel animals, realistic birds, and even some abstract sculptures but he is best known for his Raikes Bears which have been sold internationally.

Raikes is motivated by a desire to create work that will bring awareness of the uniqueness and beauty of life, and happiness to those people who see his creations. For Raikes there is a sense of accomplishment in creating work that touches people, but there is an inner peace that comes through using the creative gift given him by God. A better world comes through setting good examples and doing one's best for oneself and for others. Creating sculpture is the means by which he tries to accomplish that.

This is a very exciting time for the Raikes family. Not only are they in the midst of creating a wonderful new line of all wood posable figurine characters but they are in the process of adopting two little boys from Russia, a challenging and exciting addition to their family.

454.   Larkin: issued 1995, 5in (13cm), cast in resin, open edition.
455.   Warren: issued 1995, 5in (13cm), cast in resin, open edition.
456.   Morris: issued 1995, 5in (13cm), cast in resin, open edition.

457

459

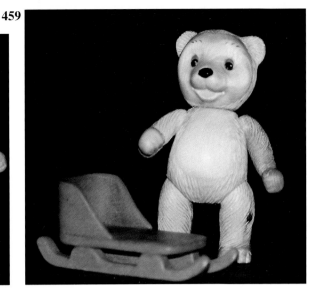

458

457.   *Gweenz:* issued 1995, 4-1/2in (11cm), cast in resin, open edition.
458.   *Willie:* issued 1995, 4-1/2in (11cm), cast in resin, open edition.
459.   *Martin:* issued 1995, 4-1/2in (11cm), cast in resin, open edition.

RUSS® BERRIE AND COMPANY

TEDDY TOWN™ COLLECTION

Russ® Berrie and Company designs and markets a vast selection of impulse gifts and toys to retail stores throughout the world. The company's core business, established in 1963, sells over 7,000 products into more than 50,000 retail outlets.

Russ® markets a diverse line of everyday and seasonal products that focuses on theme or concept groupings such as baby, home decor, lifestyles and collectibles. Individual products include stuffed animals, figurines, porcelain gifts, ceramic mugs, picture frames, kitchen magnets and stationary products.

After over thirty years of successfully selling quality bears, Russ® Berrie and Company, Inc., has put their creativity and expertise into the Teddy Town™ Collection of bear figurines. Teddy Town™ was first introduced to consumers in 1994 with ten initial styles. Since then the collection has grown to over fifty with new pieces being introduced every six months. In 1995 and 1996 a new series of the same characters with a changed face style were introduced.

The Teddy Town™ bears are made of Sculptique™, which is a high grade, molded PVC material. Each fully jointed bear stands approximately 4-3/4 inches tall. This makes them easy to pose for a variety of displays. Each bear is uniquely dressed and accessorized. Special care is taken to choose the best fabrics—like denims, corduroys, knitted sweaters, plaids, and more! Russ® has released "everyday" Teddy Town™ bears, as well as seasonal Teddy Town™ bears dressed to celebrate holidays and special occasions such as Christmas, Valentine's Day, St. Patrick's Day, Thanksgiving, and Halloween.

Russ® has a collection of Teddy Town™ figurines crafted in Sculptstone™. Each figurine is imprinted on the base with a special message commemorating a special occasion. Teddy Town™ Village is another collection of "Town Square" with open interior houses and landscaped display pieces The Teddy Town™ Collection was specially created so that teddy bear lovers and collectors could have complimentary pieces to their plush bears. The Russ® Art Studios constantly creates new ideas for trendy and traditional character bears.

TEDDY TOWN™ COLLECTION
All fully jointed Sculptique™ figurine

460

461

462

463

464

465

466

467

468

469

470

460. **Nighty Night Girl:** issued 1995, 4-3/4in (12cm), closed edition, character will be introduced in 1996 with new face style.

461. **P. J. Boy:** issued 1995, 4-3/4in (12cm), closed edition, character will be introduced in 1996 with new face style.

462. **P. J. Girl:** issued 1995, 4-3/4in (12cm), closed edition, character will be introduced in 1996 with new face style.

463. **Nurse:** issued 1995, 4 -3/4in (12cm), closed edition, character will be introduced in 1996 with new face style.

464. **Ballerina:** issued 1995, 4-3/4in (12cm), closed edition, character will be introduced in 1996 with new face style.

465. **Golfer:** issued 1995, 4-3/4in (12cm), closed edition, character will be introduced in 1996 with new face style.

466. **"I Love You":** issued 1995, 4-3/4in (12cm), closed edition, character will be introduced in 1996 with new face style.

467. **"Get Well Soon":** issued 1995, 4-3/4in (12cm), closed edition, character will be introduced in 1996 with new face style.

468. **Pilot:** issued 1995, 4 -3/4in (12cm), closed edition, character will be introduced in 1996 with new face style.

469. **Boy, "I Love You":** issued 1995, 4-3/4in (12cm), closed edition, character will be introduced in 1996 with new face style.

470. **"My First Holy Communion", Girl:** issued 1995, 4-3/4in (12cm), closed edition, character will be introduced in 1996 with new face style.

TEDDY TOWN™ COLLECTION
All fully jointed Sculptique™ figurine

471

472

473

474

475

476

477

478

479

480

481

482

483

484

471. **Sailor Girl:** issued 1995, 4-3/4in (12cm), closed edition, character will be introduced in 1996 with new face style.

472. **Sheriff:** issued 1995, 4-3/4in (12cm), closed edition, character will be introduced in 1996 with new face style.

473. **Fisherman:** issued 1995, 4-3/4in (12cm), closed edition, character will be introduced in 1996 with new face style.

474. **"Happy Birthday" Clown:** issued 1995, 4-3/4in (12cm), closed edition, character will be introduced in 1996 with new face style.

475. **"My First Holy Communion", Boy:** issued 1995, 4-3/4in (12cm), closed edition, character will be introduced in 1996 with new face style.

476. **Sunshine:** issued 1995, 4-3/4in (12cm), closed edition, character will be introduced in 1996 with new face style.

477. **Springtime Girl:** issued 1995, 4-3/4in (12cm), closed edition, character will be introduced in 1996 with new face style.

478. **Rainwear Teddy:** issued 1995, 4-3/4in (12cm), closed edition, character will be introduced in 1996 with new face style.

479. **Winter Girl:** issued 1995, 4-3/4in (12cm), closed edition, character will be introduced in 1996 with new face style.

480. **Winter Boy:** issued 1995, 4-3/4in (12cm), closed edition, character will be introduced in 1996 with new face style.

481. **Colonial Girl:** issued 1995, 4-3/4in (12cm), closed edition, character will be introduced in 1996 with new face style.

482. **Country Girl in Denim:** issued 1995, 4-3/4in (12cm), closed edition, character will be introduced in 1996 with new face style.

483. **Country Boy in Denim:** issued 1995, 4-3/4in (12cm), closed edition, character will be introduced in 1996 with new face style.

484. **Country Girl in Plaid:** issued 1995, 4-3/4in (12cm), closed edition, character will be introduced in 1996 with new face style.

TEDDY TOWN™ COLLECTION
All fully jointed Sculptique™ figurine

485

486

487

488

490

491

489

492

485. **Prep School Girl:** issued 1995, 4-3/4in (12cm), closed edition, character will be introduced in 1996 with new face style.
486. **School Boy:** issued 1995, 4-3/4in (12cm), closed edition, character will be introduced in 1996 with new face style.
487. **School Girl:** issued 1995, 4-3/4in (12cm), closed edition, character will be introduced in 1996 with new face style.
488. **Face Style:** in 1994 series 1.
489. **Top: 50th Anniversary; Bottom Left: 25th Anniversary; Wedding Bears:** issued 1995, 4in (10cm), open edition.
490. **Face Style:** in 1995 series 2.
491. **Face Style:** in 1996 series 3.
492. **Birthday Boy:** issued 1995, 6in (15cm), open edition.

TEDDY TOWN™ COLLECTION

All fully jointed Sculptique™ figurine

493

494

495

496

TEDDY TOWN™ VILLAGE

All fully jointed
Sculptique™ figurine

497

498

493. *Birthday Girl:* issued
1995, 6in (15cm),
open edition.

494. *Ballerina:* issued
1995, 6in (15cm),
open edition.

495. *Flower Shop:* issued
1995, 4in (10cm),
open edition.

496. *Hospital:* issued
1995, 4in (10cm),
open edition.

497. *Fruit Store:* issued
1995, 4in (10cm),
open edition.

498. *Honey Restaurant:*
issued 1995,
4in (10cm),
open edition.

499. *Teddy Bakery:* issued
1995, 4in (10cm),
open edition.

500. *School:* issued 1995,
4in (10cm),
open edition.

499

500

TEDDY TOWN™ VILLAGE
All fully jointed Sculptique™ figurine

502

501

504

503

501. **Top Left:** *The Baseball Game:* 1-3/4in (5cm), **School Bus:** 3 x 2in (8 x 5cm), **Bottom Left:** *In the Garden:* 2in (5cm), *Fruit Stand:* 2in (5cm), all issued 1995, open edition.
502. Completed village shown with *"Town Square"* and landscape pieces.
503. **Top Left:** *Wishing Well:* 3-3/4in (10cm), **Milk Truck:** 3 x 2in (8 x 5cm); **Bottom Left:** *Family Dinner:* 1-3/4in (5cm); *The Artist:* 2in (5cm), all issued 1995, open edition.
504. **Top:** *Village Doctor;* **Bottom Left:** *Village Nurse; "Boo-Boo" Bear:* all issued 1995, 1-1/2in (4cm), open edition.

SARAH'S ATTIC®

Sarah Schultz started her own business on the family dining room table in 1983, turning her favorite hobby into a wholesale company.

With the help of her husband, five children, and many friends, Sarah originally began to supply the family pharmacy with unique gifts to complement the country decor. When orders poured in and space ran out, the business moved to the "attic" above the pharmacy in late 1984. By mid-1989, Sarah's Attic® had expanded to four times its original size. In the fall of 1991, due to cramped quarters, Sarah's Attic was on the move once again. Sarah purchased and remodeled a former grocery store with 10,000 square feet of work area. The art room and business offices still remain in the attic.

As business expanded, so did the line, to include collectibles and wood items that complement any decor. Through all this growth and many changes, one thing remained the same—Sarah's devotion to excellent quality. Because of Sarah's devotion and because of her firm belief in love, respect and dignity, a heart

was painted on each piece as a symbol and trademark of those characteristics.

Sarah's Attic® has turned into an extremely successful company, which is no surprise to Sarah's collectors. They know that once they have purchased a Sarah's Attic® collectible, they have purchased a high-quality, original treasure of timeless value which is made with love, respect and dignity.

MICHAUD COLLECTION

In 1993, Sarah's Attic® joined forces with teddy bear artists and authorities Terry and Doris Michaud, to offer replicas of famous bears from the Michaud collection. The Michauds, pioneers in the world of collectible teddy bears, have a renowned collection of antique teddies with fascinating stories. Sarah's Attic® took the plush antique teddies and accurately captured the character of each bear in a resin figurine. The Michaud Collection is comprised of 29 resin figurines, which include single bears and additional scenes. Each bear is accompanied with a history. Even though Sarah's Attic® has retired the collection in December 1995, collectors are still seeking the figurines on the secondary market.

Sarah's Attic® introduce a figurine in 1995, for the Good Bears of the World which is an international non-profit organization that spreads love and caring to others by giving away teddy bears to hurt, abused, or traumatized children as well as lonely adults in the world. The very special bear is part of the Michaud collection. A portion of the proceeds from the sale of the "Love Heals All" figurine will be given to this charitable organization.

505

506 **507** **508**

509

LEFT to RIGHT: Top to Bottom:
505.   *Bay City Beauty:* 3-1/8in (8.31cm), issued January 1995, cast in resin, retired December 1995. *Tommy's Bear:* 2-3/4in (7cm); issued in 1993, cast in resin, retired 1995. *Michaud Bear Sign:* 2-1/2in (6cm), issued 1993, cast in resin, retired 1995. *Dowager Twins:* 2-1/2in (6cm); issued in 1993, cast in resin, retired 1995. *Second-Hand Rose:* 2-1/2in (6cm), issued in 1993, cast in resin, retired 1995. *Aunt Eunice Bear:* 2in (5cm); issued in 1993, cast in resin, retired 1995. *Me and My Shadow:* 2-1/4in (5.65cm), issued in 1993, cast in resin, retired 1995. *Just Ted Bear; Bellhop Bear; Professor Bear:* 2-1/4in (5.65cm), issued in 1993, cast in resin, retired 1995. *Irish Bear:* 2-1/2in (6cm), issued in 1993, cast in resin, retired 1995. *Proxy Bear:* 2-1/4in (5.65cm), issued January 1995, cast in resin, retired December 1995.
506.   *Witchie Bear:* 2-3/4in (7cm), cast in resin, retired 1994.
507.   *Eddie Bear:* 2-1/4in (5.65cm), cast in resin, retired 1994.
508.   *Librarian Bear:* 2-1/8in (5.31cm), cast in resin, retired 1994.
509.   *Witchie with Pot:* 3-1/2in (9cm), cast in resin, retired 1994.

510

511

512

513

LEFT to RIGHT: Top to Bottom:

510. *Irish Bear at Pub:* 3-3/4in (10cm), issued 1993, cast in resin, retired 1995.
Professor with Board: 3-5/8in (10cm), issued 1993, cast in resin, retired 1995.
Tommy with Dog: 4in (10cm), cast in resin, retired 1995. *Proxy Bear:* 2-1/4in
(5.65cm); issued January 1995, cast in resin, retired December 1995. *Aunt Eunice*
Bath Time: 4in (10cm), cast in resin, retired 1995. *Eddie with Trunk:* 2-1/4in
(5.65cm), issued 1993, cast in resin, retired 1995. *Just Ted with Mirror:* 3-1/2in
(9cm); issued 1993, cast in resin, retired 1995. *Bay City Beauty with Trunk:*
4-1/2in (11cm), cast in resin, retired December 1995. *Librarian with Desk:*
4in (10cm). issued 1993, cast in resin, retired 1995. *Bellhop/Second Hand Rose:*
3-1/4in (8.65cm); issued 1993, cast in resin, retired 1995.

511. *Dowager Twins with Couch:* 3-3/4in (10cm), retired 1994.

512. *Love Heals All* (Good Bears of the World): 2-3/8in (5.9cm), issued 1995, cast in
resin, open edition.

513. *Me and My Shadow:* 4in (10cm), retired 1994.

SCHMID

ROOSEVELT BEARS™

Schmid has been synonymous with the finest gifts and collectibles since 1932. The family-owned company remains dedicated to the same uncompromising standards of design and workmanship that have made it an industry leader for over sixty years.

Schmid has expanded considerably over the years. Today, the company boasts a number of sought-after licenses, a collection of musicals, figurines, ornaments and nursery accessories. Schmid also represents one of the most talent TOBY® award-winning miniature teddy bear artist in the world, April Whitcomb Gustafson.

Gustafson and her travelling Roosevelt Bears™ offer yet another opportunity for Schmid to expand its market. Schmid introduced six Roosevelt Bear™ figurines in 1994. The collection created quite a stir in sophisticated toy stores, as well as in miniature and collectible markets.

April Whitcomb Gustafson's name is already well-known among collectors, who generally pay up to $1500 for each of her limited edition originals. While her partnership with Schmid rep-

resents April's first venture with a manufacturer, she has actually been sculpting miniature bears since 1979.

According to April, The Roosevelt Bears™ Collection was inspired by Seymour Eaton's "Travelling Bears" stories of the early 1900s. Her own interest in creating the bears was sparked only recently with the purchase of one of Eaton's books at an antique show. The illustrations were so great, she had to recapture them in sculpture. The Roosevelt Bears™ are absolutely faithful to the original pictures, complete with the bear's incredibly detailed outfits.

This one-of-a-kind collection includes six individual sets, each featuring the 2 inch articulated Roosevelt Bears™, Teddy B (B for brown), and Teddy G (G for grey), dressed in costumes that reflect their travels around the world. Each Roosevelt Bears™ set will be packaged in a miniature steamer trunk to enhance the travelling bear theme. The bears themselves are handcrafted of resin for fine detail and entirely hand-painted. All twelve Roosevelt Bears™ were retired in December 1995.

514

514. **Top:** *Roosevelt Bears as Indians:* 2-1/4in (5.65cm); **Bottom:** *Roosevelt Bears Go Fishing:* 2in (5cm); issued 1994, cast in resin, retired in December 1995.

About the Artist:
APRIL WHITCOMB GUSTAFSON

April Whitcomb Gustafson's life-long love affair with miniature bears might never have begun. As it happens, though, a bad case of myopia is what first drew the award-winning miniature bear artist to the diminutive characters. She was nearsighted as a child, she couldn't even see the squares in the kitchen floor linoleum! April remembers, as a result, she loved tiny things, the smaller, the better—things that couldn't be appreciated unless they were held up close. Gustafson was absolutely enchanted with miniature bears.

Gustafson began collecting miniature bears at age six. Even after her poor vision was corrected with glasses a few years later, her passion for small-size bears never dimmed. By the time April graduated from college with an art degree in 1979, though, she discovered it was becoming almost impossible to find the high quality miniatures she so loved. She decided to begin moonlighting in miniatures—hand-sculpting her own bears at night in her Boylston, Massachusetts home, after returning from her 40-hour per week job as a graphic artist. Almost immediately, and largely by word-of-mouth, April's miniature bears became enormously popular among collectors around the world—selling for between $100 and $1500 each. Two of the bears have won Golden Teddy Awards. Also she was a TOBY® nominee in 1991 and TOBY® winner in 1992. Unlike any artist bears available on the market, April's original creations have the look of stuffed bears but are actually hand-sculpted of clay, painted by hand and coveted with velvet "fur."

As a long-time collector of Lowell Davis' sculptured porcelain figurines, Gustafson was familiar with the Schmid name and their reputation for quality. Gustafson approached Schmid to recreate the Roosevelt Bears™ because she knew they would do a great job. Her partnership with Schmid brought a successful collection of miniature teddy bear figurines.

515

516

517

518

519

TOP to BOTTOM:

515. *Roosevelt Bears in Traveling Suits; Roosevelt Bears as Patriots:* issued 1993, 2in (5cm), cast in resin, retired in December 1995.

516. *Roosevelt Bears In Clown Suits:* 2-1/2in (6cm); *Roosevelt Bears in Swim Suits:* 2in (5cm); issued 1993, cast in resin, retired in December 1995.

517. *Roosevelt Bears In Baseball Suits:* 2in (5cm); *Roosevelt Bears In Military Uniforms:* 2-1/4in (5.65 cm); issued 1993, cast in resin, retired in December 1995.

518. *Roosevelt Bears Fights Fires:* 2-1/8in (5.31cm); *Roosevelt Bears the Graduate:* 2-1/8in (5.31cm); issued 1994, cast in resin, retired in December 1995.

519. *Roosevelt Bears Do the Cake Walk Dance:* 2in (5cm); *Roosevelt Bears as Organ Grinders:* 2in (5cm); issued 1994, cast in resin, retired in December 1995.

STEIFF USA, L. P.

The Steiff Company was founded in 1877 by Margarete Steiff. The Steiff name is synanomous with a guarantee for the highest quality and most beautiful line of teddy bears and plush animals.

The company approached well-known artist Peter Fagan to create three resin figurines after reproductions of Steiff plush bears and their companions. These are the first and only teddy bear figurines the company has offered to collectors. The first two were introduced in 1994 and one in 1995. Each figurine measures 2-1/4 to 2-1/2 inches. These figurines are sculpted and painted with great detail. The Steiff Company only offers three teddy bear figurines at the present time. There are no plans to add more resin teddy bear figurines in the near future.

For additional information about artist Peter Fagan, see Enesco® Corporation, PennyWhistle Lane and Centimental Bears Collections.

520

521

522

520.   ***Teddy Rose*** (1925) and ***Bully Dog*** (1927): 2-1/4in (5.65cm), issued 1994, resin reproduction of Steiff bear and companion, open edition.
521.   ***Baerle 35PB*** (1904), and ***Roly Poly*** (1909): 2-1/4in (5.65cm), issued 1994, resin reproduction of Steiff bear and companion, open edition.
522.   ***Zotty*** (1951) and ***Tiger*** (1955): 2-1/2in (6cm), issued 1994, resin reproduction of Steiff bears and companion, open edition.

UNITED DESIGN® CORPORATION

TEDDY ANGELS™

Gary and Jean Clinton, both graduates of the University of Oklahoma School of Art, founded the company United Design® Corporation in Noble, Oklahoma, in 1993. Their goal was to produce figurines with a uniquely American look, a look that would reflect both the vitality and the good humor of the American perspective. A number of figurine collections: Stone Critters®, The Legend of Santa Claus™, The Legend of Little People™, the Easter Bunny Family™, and the Angels Collection™, have exemplified that perspective.

United Design® became involved with teddy bears in 1990 with the introduction of PenniBears™ by artist Penni Jo Jonas. The latest line, Teddy Angels™ was introduced in 1995. Teddy Angels™ collection is a collection of loveable teddy bear friends and little angel figurines that are inspired by authentic, antique teddy bears. Creator Penni Jo Jonas spends a great deal of time detailing each original sculpture. Once the original clay sculpture is complete, the piece is carefully delivered to the mold room. A thin layer of silicon or latex is poured over the original sculpture and the mold maker uses a air brush to blow the silicon or latex into all the fine cracks and crevices that make up the detail of each figurine. Following the mold-making process, actual casting begins. The Teddy Angels™ are cast in bonded porcelain and hand-painted. Their average size is 3 to 4 inches. Each figurine is printed on the bottom with its own special sentiment and a personal story describing each figurine's origin and mission is attached.

United Design® introduced the first edition of 18 designs in late 1994. Eight new designs was introduced in 1996. United Design® has plans to add to this collection, bringing adorable teddy characters that will capture the heart of any teddy bear figurine collector. Teddy Angels™ is sure to be highly collectible in the coming years.

*See Penni Jo Originals for information about artist Penni Jo Jonas.

523

523.   ***Cowboy Murray:*** issued 1995, 5in (13cm), cast in bonded porcelain, open edition.

524. **Sweetie:** issued 1995, 4in (10cm), cast in bonded porcelain, open edition.
525. **Ivy and Blankie:** issued 1995, 3-1/2in (9cm), cast in bonded porcelain, open edition.
526. **Murray and Little Bit:** issued 1995, 4in (10cm), cast in bonded porcelain, open edition.
527. **Murray Mending Bruin:** issued 1995, 4in (10cm), cast in bonded porcelain, open edition.
528. **Old Bear and Little Bit Reading:** issued 1995, 3in (8cm), cast in bonded porcelain, open edition
529. **Bunny's Picnic:** issued 1995, 4in (10cm), cast in bonded porcelain, open edition.
530. **Casey Tucking Honey In:** issued 1995, 3in (8cm), cast in bonded porcelain, open edition.
531. **Ivy in Garden:** issued 1995, 4in (10cm), cast in bonded porcelain, open edition.
532. **Tilli and Murray:** issued 1995, 3in (8cm), cast in bonded porcelain, open edition.
533. **Casey and Honey Reading:** issued 1996, 4in (10cm), cast in bonded porcelain, open edition.
534. **Old Bear:** issued 1995, 4-1/2in (11cm), cast in bonded porcelain, open edition.

535. **Bruin Making Valentines:** issued 1995, 3in (8cm), cast in bonded porcelain, open edition.

536. **Bruin and Bluebirds:** issued 1995, 4in (10cm), cast in bonded porcelain, open edition.

537. **Honey:** issued 1995, 3in (8cm), cast in bonded porcelain, open edition.

538. **Tilli and Doves:** issued 1995, 4in (10cm), cast in bonded porcelain, open edition.

539. **Sweetie and Santa Bear:** issued 1995, 4in (10cm), cast in bonded porcelain, open edition.

540. **Casey:** issued 1995, 3in (8cm), cast in bonded porcelain, open edition.

541. **Ivy:** issued 1995, 3-1/2in (9cm), cast in bonded porcelain, open edition.

542. **Bruin with Harp Sea Pup:** issued 1996, 3in (8cm), cast in bonded porcelain, open edition.

543. **Murray with Angel:** issued 1996, 5in (13cm), cast in bonded porcelain, open edition.

544. **Nicholas with Net of Stars:** issued 1996, 4in (10cm), cast in bonded porcelain, open edition.

545. **Old Bear and Little Bit Gardening:** issued 1996, 3in (8cm), cast in bonded porcelain, open edition.

546

547

548

546. *Sweetie with Kitty Cats:* issued 1996, 3in (8cm), cast in bonded porcelain, open edition.
547. *Rufus Helps a Bird:* issued 1996, 4in (10cm), cast in bonded porcelain, open edition.
548. *Ivy with Locket:* issued 1996, 3in (8cm), cast in bonded porcelain, open edition.

VICKILANE CREATIVE DESIGN

NIGHT BEAR-FORE CHRISTMAS COLLECTION

549

550

551

For Vicki Anderson, art has always been a primary part of life as far back as she can recall. Even as a high school student, Vicki's artwork, calligraphy and watercolors already received acclaim. She began her college education at the University of Oregon in 1970 as an art major, with her husband Ron majoring in computer science and math.

The Andersons' artistic collaboration began when they polled their talents to design and market a line of sculptures and calligraphy prints. They began marketing figurines at home. Back then the Andersons believed their little business would only be a temporary part of their lives. The Andersons sold the business in 1977 after Ron completed his ministerial studies and they were called to pastor a church in a small community.

In 1985, Ron and Vicki Anderson began to realize their study, experience and faith had prepared them for a new arena of service. They set out to make a mark in the gift and collectibles business with the founding of VickiLane, Inc. The first production building in Roseburg, Oregon, employed only ten individuals but by 1983, an additional shop was built in Springfield, Oregon which has 50 employees. Future plans include growth into a third location.

Vicki is constantly developing her skills and keeping up-to-date. Her deep appreciation for each era of art history, and an awareness of its influence on her work, help her to merge current trends with long-standing traditions.

549. *Sugar Plum Sleeping in Bed:* issued 1993, 1-3/4 x 3in (5 x 8cm), cast in resin, open edition.
550. *Grandpa and Grandma Bear:* issued 1993, 3-3/4in (10cm), cast in resin, open edition.
551. *Sparky:* issued 1993, 2-1/2in (6cm), cast in resin, open edition.

552

553

554

555

556

552. **Roseberry Sleeping by the Clock:** issued 1993, 4-3/4in (12cm), cast in resin, open edition.
553. **Christmas Tree with Teddy:** issued 1987, 3-1/2in (9cm), cast in resin, open edition.
554. **"It's Bedtime Fuzzy":** issued 1993, 3-3/4in (10 cm), cast in resin, open edition.
555. **Papa Bear with Presents:** issued 1993, 4in (10cm), cast in resin, open edition.
556. **Snowman with Bears:** issued 1993; 3-3/4in (10cm), cast in resin, open edition.

COLLECTOR CLUBS

Many collectors want to hear more about their favorite artists and companies, and collector clubs are a valuable source of information to educate the collector and enhance their interest of collecting. Nearly every club welcomes its members with a membership kit and opportunity to purchase exclusive "members-only" collectibles. Joining a club can give you a first-hand look on new release figurines and if they are retiring any figurines. Listed below are sponsored collector clubs. You may write the clubs below or visit your local collectible dealers for club information.

The Bialosky Treasury
Collector's Club
P.O. Box 258
Allendale, NJ 07401-0258

The Boyds Collection, LTD
Bearstone™ Collection
P. O. Box 4385
Gettysburg, PA 17325
(No club, but enjoy hearing from collectors)
Newsletter is available from Boyds collection dealers.

The Cavanagh Group
Coca-Cola® Heritage Collection
1000 Holcomb Woods Parkway
Roswell, Georgia 30076

The Cherished Teddies® Club
Enesco Corporation
P. O. Box 91796
Elk Grove Village, IL 60009-9179

Crystal World Collectibles
3 Borinski Drive
Lincoln Park, NJ 07035
(201) 633-0707

Franklin Mint Collectors Society
The Franklin Mint
Franklin Center, PA 19091

Great American® Collector's Club
Great American® Taylor
Collectibles Corp.
P.O. Box 428
Aberdeen, NC, 28315

Lucy & Me® Collecting Network
Attn: CB
P. O. Box 31265
Omaha, NE 68131-0265

Muffy Vanderbear Club
North American Bear Co., Inc.
401 N. Wabash, Suite 500
Chicago, IL 60611

Nevenschwander Artworks
Bread n' Butter Bears
Collectors Club
Rt. 1, Box 1596
Stella, MO 64867
(417) 364-7623

PenniBears™ Collectors Club
Penni Jo's Originals LTD
1413 N. E. Lincoln Ave.
Moore, OK 73160
(405) 799-0006

Peter Fagan
Colour Box Collector's Club
Orchard Estate, Lauder,
Berwickshire, TD 2 6RH

Robert Raikes Collectors Club
Raikes Originals
P.O. Box 82
MT. Shasta, CA 96067
(916) 926-4872

Sarah's Attic® Forever Friends
Collector's Club
126 1/2 WestBroad Street
P.O. Box 448
Chesaning, MI 48616
(800) 437-4363

MAGAZINES AND PERIODICALS

COLLECTOR INFORMATION BUREAU
CIB REPORT AND SHOWCASE
5060 Shoreline Rd., Suite 200
Barrington, IL 60010
(708) 842-2200

COLLECTORS NEWS
P.O. Box 156
Grundy Center, Iowa 50-638
(319) 834-6981

COLLECTOR'S EDITION
COLLECTOR COMMUNICATION CORP.
P.O. Box 1948
Marion, OH 43305
800 347-6969

COLLECTOR'S MART
KRAUSE PUBLICATION
700 E. State Street
Iola, WI 54990
800 258-0929

FIGURINES & COLLECTIBLES
COWLES MAGAZINE
6405 Flank Drive
Harrisburg, PA 17112
800 435-9610

TEDDY BEAR & FRIENDS
COWLES MAGAZINE
6405 Flank Drive
Harrisburg, PA 17112
800 435-9610

TEDDY BEAR REVIEW
COLLECTOR COMMUNICATION CORP.
P.O. Box 1948
Marion, OH 43305
800 347-6969

ABOUT THE AUTHOR

Georigia born sculptor, freelance writer, teddy bear collector Jesse Murray is known for his unique limited edition sawdust teddy bear figurines. His work draws world-wide collectors and has been featured in several art and collector publications.

Jesse has worked as a professional sculptor for ten years, designing teddy bear figurines in many mediums. His interest in plush and figurines was sparked as a child. Today Jesse can still remember molding teddy bears from play dough and papier-mâché. Jesse knew from an early age that he wanted to become a teddy bear artist.

After indepth research on the world-wide teddy bear figurine industry, Jesse has admired, studied and collected many mediums used by artists and companies in creating teddy bear figurines.

He sees a growing interest in collecting teddy bear figurines in the coming years, which is sure to bring about new teddy bear collections to the figurine industry.

PRICE INDEX 1995-1996

This index includes the most widely produced and sold teddy bear figurines in todays collectible market as well as the secondary market. This index is based on company information and research from several independent market advisors.

How to Read the Price Guide:

The following abbreviations are used to identify edition size and status:

LD = LIMITED EDITION   **CL** = CLOSED   **NA** = NOT AVAILABLE

OP = OPEN   **RT** = RETIRED   **UD** = UNDISCLOSED

YR ISS = YEAR OF ISSUE (LIMITED TO CALENDAR YEAR)

SUSP = SUSPENDED

Identification Of Entry Parts:

Company   Figurine Collection

Enesco® Corporation – CHERISHED TEDDIES®

RELEASE YEAR	FIGURINE	ARTIST	EDITION	ISSUE	QUOTE
1992-43-001	Signage Plaque - 951005	P. Hillman	OP	15.00	15.00

Year Series   Title   Item #   Artist   Edition   Issue   Secondary Market
Issued   Price

ANNA-PERENNA® PORCELAIN, INC. – ADORABLES™ COLLECTION

RELEASE YEAR	FIGURINE	ARTIST	EDITION	ISSUE	QUOTE
1989-01-701	Toy Box	P. Fagan	RT 1994	25.00	35.00
1989-01-702	Holiday Bear	P. Fagan	RT 1994	25.00	35.00
1989-01-703	Highland Laddie	P. Fagan	RT 1994	11.00	20.00
1989-01-704	The Academic	P. Fagan	RT 1994	25.00	50.00
1989-01-705	Lap of Luxury	P. Fagan	RT-1994	19.80	25.00
1989-01-706	Artistic License	P. Fagan	RT-1994	19.80	25.00
1989-01-707	The Quick Life	P. Fagan	RT-1994	45.00	50.00
1989-01-716	Bruno	P. Fagan	RT-1994	11.00	15.00
1989-01-717	Humphrey	P. Fagan	RT-1994	11.00	15.00
1989-01-718	Johann	P. Fagan	RT-1994	4.00	8.00
1989-01-719	Theodore	P. Fagan	RT-1994	4.00	8.00
1989-01-720	Blue Scarf	P. Fagan	RT-1994	4.00	8.00
1989-01-721	Red Scarf	P. Fagan	RT-1994	4.00	8.00
1989-01-722	Fluffy	P. Fagan	RT-1994	4.00	8.00
1989-01-723	Jonathan	P. Fagan	RT-1994	6.00	12.00
1989-01-724	Peregrine	P. Fagan	RT-1994	6.00	12.00
1989-01-725	Teddy Robinson	P. Fagan	RT-1994	7.50	14.00
1989-01-726	Christopher Bear	P. Fagan	RT-1994	10.00	20.00
1989-01-727	Dickie Bear	P. Fagan	RT-1994	10.00	20.00
1989-01-728	Gustav Von Bruin	P. Fagan	RT-1994	8.00	16.00
1989-01-729	August String Bear	P. Fagan	RT-1994	10.00	20.00
1989-01-730	Robert	P. Fagan	RT-1994	8.00	16.00
1989-01-731	Peter Bear	P. Fagan	RT-1994	7.50	14.00
1989-01-732	Fisherman's Friend	P. Fagan	RT-1994	35.00	50.00
1989-01-733	Home Movie	P. Fagan	RT-1994	25.00	35.00
1990-01-734	Broderick	P. Fagan	RT-1994	7.50	14.00
1990-01-735	Bernard	P. Fagan	RT-1994	7.50	14.00
1990-01-736	Writing Home	P. Fagan	RT-1994	18.50	25.00
1990-01-739	Train Spotter	P. Fagan	RT-1994	15.00	30.00
1990-01-738	Starch and Press	P. Fagan	RT-1994	29.50	40.00
1990-01-739	Tuck Box	P. Fagan	RT-1994	15.00	25.00
1990-01-464	School Days	P. Fagan	RT-1994	35.00	40.00
1991-01-752	Barrow Boy	P. Fagan	RT-1994	35.00	45.00
1991-01-753	Ben	P. Fagan	RT-1994	7.50	12.50
1991-01-754	First Aid Post	P. Fagan	RT-1994	30.00	35.00
1991-01-755	Irvine	P. Fagan	RT-1994	7.50	12.50
1991-01-756	Mr. Perkins	P. Fagan	RT-1994	7.50	12.50
1991-01-757	Chocolate Chip	P. Fagan	RT-1994	7.50	12.50
1991-01-758	Shiner	P. Fagan	RT-1994	4.00	8.00
1991-01-759	Tinker Thomas	P. Fagan	RT-1994	4.00	8.00
1991-01-760	Derek	P. Fagan	RT-1994	15.00	20.00
1991-01-761	Baron Von Berne	P. Fagan	RT-1994	15.00	20.00
1991-01-762	Brodie	P. Fagan	RT-1994	15.00	20.00
1991-01-763	Educating Timmy	P. Fagan	RT-1994	45.00	55.00

THE BIALOSKY TREASURY – BIALOSKY TREASURY FIGURINES

RELEASE YEAR	FIGURINE	ARTIST	EDITION	ISSUE	QUOTE
1995-01-001	Captain Cockpit	Bialosky	LD-10,000	18.00	18.00
1995-01-002	Captain Cruiser	Bialosky	LD-10,000	18.00	18.00
1995-01-003	Bialosky (Fisherman)	Bialosky	LD-10,000	18.00	18.00
1995-01-004	Rose Petal and Marcel	Bialosky	LD-10,000	18.00	18.00
1996-01-005	Elizabeth and Suzette	Bialosky	LD-10,000	18.00	18.00
1996-01-006	Cinnamon and Nutmeg	Bialosky	LD-10,000	18.00	18.00

BOYDS COLLECTION LTD. – THE BEARSTONE™ COLLECTION

RELEASE YEAR	FIGURINE	ARTIST	EDITION	ISSUE	QUOTE
1993-01-001	Bailey Bear with Suitcase (old version) 2000	G. M. Lowenthal	RE	14.20	20-50.00
1993-01-002	Bailey Bear with Suitcase (revised version) 2000	G. M. Lowenthal	OP	14.20	14.20-55
1993-01-003	Bailey Bear with Suitcase (prototype) 2000	G. M. Lowenthal	RT	14.20	75.00
1993-01-004	Simone De Bearvoire and Her Mom 2001	G. M. Lowenthal	OP	14.20	14.20-49
1993-01-005	Neville...The Bedtime Bear 2002	G. M. Lowenthal	OP	14.20	14.20-49
1993-01-006	Arthur...with Red Scarf 2003-03	G. M. Lowenthal	RT-12/94	14.20	14.20-49
1993-01-007	Arthur...with Green Scarf 2003-04	G. M. Lowenthal	RT-12/93	10.50	100.00
1993-01-008	Grenville...with Red Scarf 2003-08	G. M. Lowenthal	RT-12/95	10.50	55.00
1993-01-009	Victoria...The Lady 2004	G. M. Lowenthal	OP	18.40	18.40-57
1993-01-010	Moriarty-The Bear in the Cat Suit 2005	G. M. Lowenthal	RT-12/95	13.75	13.75-44
1993-01-011	Bailey in the Orchard 2006	G. M. Lowenthal	OP	14.20	14.20-49
1993-01-012	Wilson with Love Sonnet 2007	G. M. Lowenthal	OP	12.60	12.60-60
1993-01-013	Father Chrisbear and Son 2008	G. M. Lowenthal	RT-12/93	15.00	100.00
1993-01-016	Christian by the Sea 2012	G. M. Lowenthal	OP	14.20	14.20-45
1994-01-017	Bailey's Birthday 2014	G. M. Lowenthal	OP	15.95	15.95
1994-01-018	Justina & M. Harrison 2015	G. M. Lowenthal	OP	26.25	26.25
1994-01-019	Grenville & Beatrice...Best Friends 2016	G. M. Lowenthal	OP	26.25	26.25
1994-01-020	Bailey & Wixie To Have and To Hold 2017	G. M. Lowenthal	OP	15.75	15.75
1994-01-021	Bailey & Emily...Forever Friends 2018	G. M. Lowenthal	OP	34.00	34.00
1994-01-022	Sherlock & Watson-In Disguise 2019	G. M. Lowenthal	OP	15.75	15.75
1994-01-023	Wilson at the Beach 2020-06	G. M. Lowenthal	OP	15.75	15.75
1994-01-024	Bailey at the Beach 2020-09	G. M. Lowenthal	RT-12/95	15.75	15.75
1994-01-025	Juliette Angel Bear (ivory) 2029-10	G. M. Lowenthal	RT-12/95	12.60	12.60
1994-01-026	Clarence Angel Bear (rust) 2029-11	G. M. Lowenthal	RT-12/95	12.60	12.60
1994-01-027	Grenville the Santabear 2030	G. M. Lowenthal	OP	14.20	14.20
1993-01-028	Grenville & Neville...The Sign 2099	G. M. Lowenthal	OP	15.75	15.75
1993-01-029	Grenville & Neville...The Sign (prototype) 2099	G. M. Lowenthal	RT	15.75	100.00
1994-01-030	Wilson the Perfesser 2222	G. M. Lowenthal	OP	16.25	16.25
1994-01-031	Ted & Teddy 2223	G. M. Lowenthal	OP	15.75	15.75
1994-01-032	Homer on the Plate 2225	G. M. Lowenthal	OP	15.75	15.75
1994-01-034	Sebastian's Prayer 2227	G. M. Lowenthal	OP	16.25	16.25
1994-01-037	Clara...The Nurse 2231	G. M. Lowenthal	OP	16.25	16.25
1994-01-038	Grenville...The Graduate 2233	G. M. Lowenthal	OP	16.25	16.25
1994-01-039	Kringle & Bailey with List 2235	G. M. Lowenthal	OP	14.20	14.20
1994-01-040	Elgin the Elf Bear 2236	G. M. Lowenthal	OP	14.20	14.20
1994-01-044	Edmond & Bailey...Gathering Holly 2240	G. M. Lowenthal	OP	24.25	24.25
1994-01-045	Elliot & the Tree 2241	G. M. Lowenthal	OP	16.25	16.25
1994-01-046	Elliot & Snowbeary 2242	G. M. Lowenthal	OP	15.25	15.25
1994-01-048	Knute & The Gridiron 2245	G. M. Lowenthal	OP	16.25	16.25
1994-01-049	Agatha & Shelly-Scaredy Cat 2246	G. M. Lowenthal	OP	16.25	16.25
1995-01-050	Hop-a-Long...The Deputy 2247	G. M. Lowenthal	OP	14.20	14.20
1995-01-051	Otis...The Fisherman 2249-06	G. M. Lowenthal	OP	15.75	15.75
1995-01-052	Bailey...The Baker with Sweetie Pie 2254	G. M. Lowenthal	OP	12.60	12.60
1995-01-053	Miss Bruin & Bailey The Lesson 2259	G. M. Lowenthal	OP	16.25	16.25
1995-01-054	Bailey...The Honeybear 2260	G. M. Lowenthal	OP	16.25	16.25
1995-01-055	Otis...Taxtime 2262	G. M. Lowenthal	OP	16.25	16.25
1995-01-056	Grenville & Knife Football Buddies 2255	G. M. Lowenthal	OP	20.00	20.00
1995-01-057	Wilson the Wonderful Wizard of WUZ 2261	G. M. Lowenthal	OP	15.25	15.25
1995-01-058	Union Jack Love Letters 2263	G. M. Lowenthal	OP	19.00	19.00
1995-01-059	Grenville The Storyteller 2265	G. M. Lowenthal	LD 1995	49.00	65.00
1995-01-060	Angelica the Guardian 2266	G. M. Lowenthal	OP	18.50	18.50
1995-01-061	Simone & Bailey Helping Hand 2267	G. M. Lowenthal	OP	26.00	26.00
1995-01-062	Bailey The Cheerleader 2268	G. M. Lowenthal	OP	16.25	16.25
1995-01-063	Emma The Witchy Bear 2269	G. M. Lowenthal	OP	17.50	17.50
1995-01-064	Neville as Joseph 2401	G. M. Lowenthal	OP	15.00`	15.00
1995-01-065	Theresa as Mary 2402	G. M. Lowenthal	OP	15.00	15.00
1995-01-066	Baldwin as the Child 2403	G. M. Lowenthal	OP	15.00	15.00
1995-01-067	The Stage (Peace on Earth) 2425 The School Pageant	G. M. Lowenthal	OP	34.50	34.50

CAST ART INDUSTRIES – CUDDL'SOMES™

RELEASE YEAR	FIGURINE	ARTIST	EDITION	ISSUE	QUOTE
1995-01-CS001	Cuddl'somes™ Logo	K. Haynes/S. & G. Hackett	OP	15.00	15.00
1995-01-CS100	Friends	K. Haynes/S. & G. Hackett	OP	11.00	11.00
1995-01-CS101	House Call	K. Haynes/S. & G. Hackett	OP	19.50	19.50
1995-01-CS102	Scare Bear	K. Haynes/S. & G. Hackett	OP	25.00	25.00
1995-01-CS103	Jolly Roger	K. Haynes/S. & G. Hackett	OP	17.00	17.00
1995-01-CS104	Baby on Board	K. Haynes/S. & G. Hackett	OP	17.00	17.00
1995-01-CS105	Motherhood	K. Haynes/S. & G. Hackett	OP	25.00	25.00
1995-01-CS106	Perfect Ten	K. Haynes/S. & G. Hackett	OP	11.00	11.00
1995-01-CS107	First Step (Mini)	K. Haynes/S. & G. Hackett	OP	9.00	9.00
1995-01-CS108	Sugar Ray (Mini)	K. Haynes/S. & G. Hackett	OP	9.00	9..00
1995-01-CS109	Touchdown Bear (Mini)	K. Haynes/S. & G. Hackett	OP	9.00	9.00
1995-01-CS110	Rah Rah (Mini)	K. Haynes/S. & G. Hackett	OP	9.00	9.00
1995-01-CS111	Sparky	K. Haynes/S. & G. Hackett	OP	9.00	9.00
1995-01-CS112	School Days (Mini)	K. Haynes/S. & G. Hackett	OP	9.00	9.00
1995-01-CS113	Happy Bearday (Mini)	K. Haynes/S. & G. Hackett	OP	9.00	9.00
1995-01-CS114	Cubby	K. Haynes/S. & G. Hackett	OP	17.00	17.00
1995-01-CS115	Eddie Rickenbear	K. Haynes/S. & G. Hackett	OP	18.00	18.00
1995-01-CS116	Splash	K. Haynes/S. & G. Hackett	OP	18.00	18.00
1995-01-CS117	Ice Dancer	K. Haynes/S. & G. Hackett	OP	17.00	17.00
1995-01-CS118	Dress Up	K. Haynes/S. & G. Hackett	OP	17.00	17.00
1995-01-CS119	Dear Santa	K. Haynes/S. & G. Hackett	OP	25.00	25.00
1995-01-CS120	Beary Christmas	K. Haynes/S. & G. Hackett	OP	17.00	17.00
1995-01-CS121	Tiny Tim (Mini)	K. Haynes/S. & G. Hackett	OP	9.00	9.00
1995-01-CS122	Roosevelt	K. Haynes/S. & G. Hackett	OP	29.00	29.00
1995-01-CS123	Rupert	K. Haynes/S. & G. Hackett	OP	17.00	17.00
1995-01-CS124	Snuggles	K. Haynes/S. & G. Hackett	OP	9.00	9.00
1995-01-CS125	Sundance	K. Haynes/S. & G. Hackett	OP	29.00	29.00
1995-01-CS126	Winchester	K. Haynes/S. & G. Hackett	OP	19.50	19.50
1995-01-CS127	Howdy (Mini)	K. Haynes/S. & G. Hackett	OP	9.00	9.00
1995-01-CS128	Side Kick	K. Haynes/S. & G. Hackett	OP	25.00	25.00
1995-01-CS129	First Mate	K. Haynes/S. & G. Hackett	OP	17.00	17.00
1995-01-CS130	Hucklebeary	K. Haynes/S. & G. Hackett	OP	17.00	17.00
1995-01-CS131	Archibald	K. Haynes/S. & G. Hackett	OP	15.00	15.00
1995-01-CS132	Tatters	K. Haynes/S. & G. Hackett	OP	15.00	15.00
1995-01-CS141	We Need Love	K. Haynes/S. & G. Hackett	OP	15.00	15.00
1995-01-CS142	Lost and Lonely	K. Haynes/S. & G. Hackett	OP	15.00	15.00
1995-01-CS143	Keystone	K. Haynes/S. & G. Hackett	OP	17.00	17.00
1995-01-CS144	Abbie Lou	K. Haynes/S. & G. Hackett	OP	17.00	17.00
1995-01-CS151	Big Big Hug	K. Haynes/S. & G. Hackett	OP	17.00	17.00
1995-01-CS152	Tea for Two	K. Haynes/S. & G. Hackett	OP	20.00	20.00
1995-01-CS153	Two A.M. Feeding	K. Haynes/S. & G. Hackett	OP	18.00	18.00
1995-01-CS154	At the Malt Shop	K. Haynes/S. & G. Hackett	OP	18.00	18.00
1995-01-CS155	The Happy Couple	K. Haynes/S. & G. Hackett	OP	15.00	15.00
1995-01-CS156	Bacon & Eggs	K. Haynes/S. & G. Hackett	OP	15.00	15.00

CAVAVAGH GROUP INTERNATIONAL – COCA-COLA® HERITAGE COLLECTION

RELEASE YEAR	FIGURINE	ARTIST	EDITION	ISSUE	QUOTE
1994-01-22004	Skating Polar Bear (Musical)	In-House	LD	18.00	18.00
1994-01-23001	Two Polar Bears on Ice (Musical)	In-House	OP	45.00	45.00
1994-01-23002	Two Polar Bears on Ice	In-House	OP	25.00	25.00
1994-01-23003	Eight Polar Bears	In-House	LD15,000	125.00	125.00
1994-01-23005	Eight Polar Bears (Musical)	In-House	LD15,000	150.00	150.00
1994-01-42551	"Always Cool" Polar Bear	In-House	LD	55.00	55.00
1995-01-23011	Polar Bear Family (Musical)	In-House	OP	50.00	50.00

CRYSTAL WORLD® – TEDDYLAND

RELEASE YEAR	FIGURINE	ARTIST	EDITION	ISSUE	QUOTE
1987-01-552	Loving Teddies	N. Mulargia	OP	99.50	99.50
1987-01-562	Sailing Teddies	N. Mulargia	OP	105.00	105.00
1987-01-580	Teddy Bear Christmas	N. Mulargia	OP	95.00	95.00
1987-01-589	Skiing Teddy	R. Nakai	OP	52.50	52.50
1987-01-590	Beach Teddies	N. Mulargia	OP	95.00	95.00
1988-01-600	Teddy Family	N. Mulargia	OP	57.50	57.50
1988-01-602	Teddies at Eight	N. Mulargia	OP	105.00	105.00
1988-01-603	Touring Teddies	R. Nakai	OP	105.00	105.00
1989-01-635	Happy Birthday Teddy	R. Nakai	OP	52.50	52.50
1989-01-637	Golfing Teddies	R. Nakai	OP	105.00	105.00
1989-01-645	Speedboat Teddies	R. Nakai	OP	79.50	79.50
1990-01-660	Small Loving Teddies	N. Mulargia	OP	64.50	64.50
1990-01-676	Storytime Teddies	T. Suzuki	OP	79.50	79.50
1991-01-709	Swinging Teddies	N. Mulargia	OP	105.00	105.00

CRYSTAL WORLD® – TEDDYLAND

RELEASE YEAR	FIGURINE	ARTIST	EDITION	ISSUE	QUOTE
1991-01-717	Santa Bear Christmas	T. Suzuki	OP	75.00	75.00
1991-01-718	Santa Bear Sleighrider	T. Suzuki	OP	79.00	79.00
1991-01-719	Play it again Ted	T. Suzuki	OP	63.00	63.00
1991-01-741	Gumball Teddy	T. Suzuki	OP	59.00	59.00
1992-01-746	Patriotic Teddy	N. Mulargia	OP	39.95	39.95
1992-01-758	Merry Christmas Teddy	T. Suzuki	OP	57.50	57.50
1992-01-794	Billiard Buddies	T. Suzuki	OP	69.00	69.00
1992-01-803	Ice Cream Teddies	N. Mulargia	OP	63.00	63.00
1992-01-804	Small Beach Teddies	N. Mulargia	OP	68.00	68.00
1992-01-861	Black Jack Teddies	N. Mulargia	OP	105.00	105.00
1993-01-864	Flower Teddy	T. Suzuki	OP	47.50	47.50
1995-01-895	Fly a Kite Teddy	R. Nakai	OP	40.95	40.95
1995-01-896	Compubear	R. Nakai	OP	63.00	63.00

DEPARTMENT 56, INC.® – UPSTAIRS DOWNSTAIRS BEARS™

RELEASE YEAR	FIGURINE	ARTIST	EDITION	ISSUE	QUOTE
1994-01-2000-1	Henrietta's Tea Party	C. Lawson	LD5600	75.00	95.00
1994-01-2001-0	Mr. Frederick "Freddy" Pumphrey Bosworth	C. Lawson	OP	25.00	25.00
1994-01-2002-8	Mrs. Henrietta Bosworth	C. Lawson	OP	25.00	25.00
1994-01-2003-6	Kitty Bosworth	C. Lawson	OP	16.00	16.00
1994-01-2004-4	Henry Bosworth	C. Lawson	OP	12.00	12.00
1994-01-2005-2	Alice Bosworth	C. Lawson	OP	12.00	12.00
1994-01-2006-0	Baby Arthur Bosworth	C. Lawson	OP	16.00	16.00
1994-01-2007-9	Barker, The Butler	C. Lawson	OP	25.00	25.00
1994-01-2008-7	Nanny Maybold	C. Lawson	OP	25.00	25.00
1994-01-2009-5	Flora Mardle	C. Lawson	OP	25.00	25.00
1994-01-2010-9	Mrs. Bumble	C. Lawson	OP	25.00	25.00
1994-01-2011-7	Winston	C. Lawson	OP	25.00	25.00
1994-01-2012-5	Polly	C. Lawson	OP	16.00	16.00
1994-01-2013-3	Teddy Marshbanks	C. Lawson	OP	12.50	12.50
1994-01-2014-1	Kitty & Binkie Springtime Romance	C. Lawson	OP	27.50	27.50
1994-01-2015-0	Henry & Alice Bosworth, The Easter EggHunt	C. Lawson	OP	25.00	25.00
1994-01-2016-8	Daphne Bonnett Pretty as a Picture	C. Lawson	OP	20.00	20.00
1994-01-2017-6	Henrietta Bosworth, The Easter Bonnet	C. Lawson	OP	27.50	27.50
1994-01-2018-4	Freddy Boswoth Ready for a Spin	C. Lawson	OP	25.00	25.00
1994-01-2019-2	Polly, Spring Flowers	C. Lawson	OP	20.00	20.00
1994-01-2020-6	Flora Mardle, The Artist	C. Lawson	OP	25.00	25.00
1994-01-2021-4	Mr. Bodicoat Morning Delivery	C. Lawson	OP	25.00	25.00
1994-01-2122-2	Miss Creedle, Time for Lessons	C. Lawson	OP	25.00	25.00
1994-01-2123-0	Betsy Sweetcroft, Going Out for Tea	C. Lawson	OP	12.50	12.50
1994-01-2024-9	Nanny & Baby Arthur Off to the Park	C. Lawson	OP	45.00	45.00
1995-01-2025-7	Henry Brings Home the Presents	C. Lawson	OP	22.50	22.50
1995-01-2026-5	Henry & Alice, Building a Snowbear	C. Lawson	OP	30.00	30.00
1995-01-2027-3	Henry & Alice, Finding Treats	C. Lawson	OP	25.00	25.00
1995-01-2028-1	Alice Meeting the Christmas Fairy	C. Lawson	OP	27.50	27.50
1995-01-2029-0	Kitty Cuts a Figure 8	C. Lawson	OP	20.00	20.00
1995-01-2030-3	Henry & Alice Hanging Garland	C. Lawson	OP	32.50	32.50
1995-01-2031-1	Nanny & Arthur Christmas Shopping	C. Lawson	OP	27.50	27.50

DEPARTMENT 56, INC.® – CLASSIC FURNITURE COLLECTION

RELEASE YEAR	FIGURINE	ARTIST	EDITION	ISSUE	QUOTE
1994-01-2050-8	Piecrust Table	C. Lawson	OP	50.00	50.00
1994-01-2051-6	Queen Ann Chair	C. Lawson	OP	85.00	85.00
1994-01-2052-4	Chippendale Highboy	C. Lawson	OP	85.00	85.00
1994-01-2053-2	Chippendale Mirror	C. Lawson	OP	40.00	40.00
1994-01-2054-0	Spiral Staircase	C. Lawson	OP	200.00	200.00
1994-01-2055-9	Classic Oldtime Stove	C. Lawson	OP	50.00	50.00
1994-01-2056-7	Wrought Iron Park Bench	C. Lawson	OP	45.00	45.00

ENESCO® CORPORATION – CHERISHED TEDDIES®

RELEASE YEAR	FIGURINE	ARTIST	EDITION	ISSUE	QUOTE
1992-43-001	Signage Plaque - 951005	P. Hillman	OP	15.00	15.00
1992-43-002	Nathaniel & Nellie "It's Twice As Nice With You" 950513	P. Hillman	OP	30.00	30.00
1992-43-003	Camille "I'd Be Lost Without You" 950424`	P. Hillman	OP	20.00	20.00
1992-43-004	Jasmine "You Have Touched My Heart" 950475	P. Hillman	OP	22.50	22.50
1992-43-005	Blossom & Beth "Friends Are Never Far Apart" Musical 950645	P. Hillman	OP	60.00	60.00
1992-43-006	Christopher "Old Friends Are The Best Friends" 950483	P. Hillman	OP	50.00	50.00
1992-43-007	Jeremy "Friends Like You Are Precious And Few" 950521	P. HIllman	RT95	15.00	30.00

136

Release Year	Figurine	Artist	Edition	Issue	Quote
1992-43-008	Zachary "Yesterday's Memories Are Today's Treasures" 950491	P. Hillman	OP	30.00	30.00
1992-43-009	Mandy "I Love You Just The Way You Are" 950572	P. Hillman	RT95	15.00	13.00
1992-43-010	Benji "Life Is Sweet, Enjoy" 950548	P. Hillman	RT95	13.50	27.00
1992-43-011	Anna "Hooray For You" 950459	P. Hillman	OP	22.50	22.50
1992-43-012	Beth "Bear Hugs" 950637	P. Hillman	RT95	17.50	35.00
1992-43-013	Sara "Lov Ya", Jacki "Hugs & Kisses", Karen "Best Buddy" 950432	P. Hillman	OP	10.00	10.00
1992-43-104	Joshua "Love Repairs All" 950556	P. Hillman	OP	20.00	20.00
1992-43-105	Katie "A Friend Always Knows When You Need A Hug" 950440	P. Hillman	OP	20.00	20.00
1992-43-016	Theodore, Smantha & Tyler "Friends Come In All Sizes" 950505	P. Hillman	OP	20.00	20.00
1992-43-017	Blossom & Beth "Friends Are Never Far Apart" 950564	P. Hillman	OP	50.00	50.00
1992-43-018	Theordore, Samantha & Tyler (9") "Friends Come In All Sizes" 951196	P. Hillman	OP	130.00	130.00
1992-43-019	Mary, Baby & Joseph "A Baby Is God's Gift of Love" 950688	P. Hillman	OP	35.00	35.00
1992-43-020	Creche & Quilt 951218	P. Hillman	OP	50.00	50.00
1992-43-021	Richard "My Gift Is Loving", Edward "My Gift Is Caring", Wilbur "My Gift Is Sharing" 950718	P. Hillman	OP	55.00	55.00
1992-43-022	Angie "I Brought The Star" 951137	P. Hillman	OP	15.00	15.00
1992-43-023	Sammy "Little Lambs Are In My Care" 950726	P. Hillman	OP	17.50	17.50
1992-43-024	Beth "Happy Holidays, Deer Friend" 950807	P. Hillman	OP	22.50	22.50
1992-43-025	Beth "Happy Holidays, Deer Friend" (Musical) 950816	P. Hillman	OP	60.00	60.00
1992-43-026	Charlie "The Spirit of Friendship Warms The Heart" 950742	P. Hillman	OP	22.50	22.50
1992-43-027	Jacob "Wishing For Love" 950734	P. Hillman	OP	22.50	22.50
1992-43-028	Theordore, Samantha & Tyler "Friendship Weathers All Storms" 950769	P. Hillman	OP	20.00	20.00
1992-43-029	Steven "A Season Filled With Sweetness" 951129	P. Hillman	OP	20.00	20.00
1992-43-030	Douglas "Let's Be Friends" 950661	P. Hillman	RT95	20.00	40.00
1993-43-031	Marie "Friendship Is A Special Treat" 910767	P. Hillman	OP	20.00	20.00
1993-43-032	Priscilla "Love Surrounds Our Friendship" 910724	P. Hillman	OP	15.00	15.00
1993-43-033	Timothy "A Friend Is Forever" 910740	P. Hillman	OP	15.00	15.00
1993-43-034	Amy "Hearts Quilted With Love" 910732	P. Hillman	OP	13.50	13.50
1993-43-035	Michael & Michelle "Friendship Is A Cozy Feeling" 910775	P. Hillman	OP	30.00	30.00
1993-43-036	Abigail "Inside We're All The Same" 900362	P. Hillman	OP	16.00	16.00
1993-43-037	Henrietta "A Basketful of Wings" 910686	P. Hillman	SUSP	22.00	45-75.00
1993-43-038	Molly "Friendship Softens A Bumpy Ride" 910759	P. Hillman	OP	30.00	30.00
1993-43-039	Charity "I Found A Friend in Ewe" 910678	P. Hillman	SUSP	20.00	45-50.00
1993-43-043	Daisy "Friendship Blossoms With Love" 910651	P. Hillman	SUSP	15.00	36-120.00
1993-43-041	Heidi & David "Special Friends" 910708	P. Hillman	OP	25.00	25.00
1993-43-042	Chelsea "Good Friends Are A Blessing" 910694	P. Hillman	RT95	15.00	45.00
1993-43-043	Baby Blocks CRT004	P. Hillman	OP	40.00	40.00
1993-43-044	Baby "Cradled With Love" 911356	P. Hillman	OP	16.50	16.50
1993-43-045	"Beary Special One" Age 1 911348	P. Hillman	OP	13.50	13.50
1993-43-046	"Two Sweet Two Bear" Age 2 911321	P. Hillman	OP	13.50	13.50
1993-43-047	"Three Cheers For You" Age 3 911313	P. Hillman	OP	15.00	15.00
1993-43-048	"Unfolding Happy Wishes For You" Age 4 911305	P. Hillman	OP	15.00	15.00
1993-43-049	"Color Me Five" Age 5 911291	P. Hillman	OP	15.00	15.00
1993-43-050	"Chalking Up Six Wishes" Age 6 911283	P. Hillman	OP	16.50	16.50
1993-43-051	Patrick "Thank You For A Friend That's True" 911410	P. Hillman	OP	18.50	18.50
1993-43-052	Patrice "Thank You For The Sky So Blue" 911429	P. Hillman	OP	18.50	18.50
1993-43-053	"Thank You For A Friend That's True" (Musical) 914304	P. Hillman	OP	37.50	37.50
1993-43-054	"Thank You For The Sky So Blue" (Musical) 914312	P. Hillman	OP	37.50	37.50
1993-43-055	Thomas "Chuggin' Along", Jonathon "Sail With Me", Harrison "We're Going Places" 911739	P. Hillman	OP	15.00	15.00

RELEASE YEAR	FIGURINE	ARTIST	EDITION	ISSUE	QUOTE
1993-43-056	Tracie & Nichole "Side By Side With Friends" 911372	P. Hillman	OP	35.00	35.00
1993-43-057	Freda & Tina "Our Friendship Is A Perfect Blend" 911747	P. Hillman	OP	35.00	35.00
1993-43-058	Robbie & Rachel "Love Bears All Things" 911402	P. Hillman	OP`	27.50	27.50
1993-43-059	"Cradled With Love" (Musical) 914320	P. Hillman	OP	60.00	60.00
1993-43-060	Alice "Cozy Warm Wishes Coming Your Way" Dated 1993 912875	P. Hillman	YR.ISS.	17.50	25-55.00
1993-43-061	Alice "Cozy Warm Wishes Coming Your Way" (9") 903620	P. Hillman	SUSP	100.00	100.00
1993-43-062	"Sharing The Season Together" (Musical) 912964	P. Hillman	OP	40.00	40.00
1993-43-063	Hans "Friends In Toyland" 912956	P. Hillman	OP	20.00	20.00
1993-43-064	Carolyn "Wishing You All Good Things" 912921	P. Hillman	OP	22.50	22.50
1993-43-065	"Our Friendship Weathers All Storms" (Musical) 903337	P. Hillman	OP	60.00	60.00
1993-43-066	Theodore, Smantha & Tyler "Friendship Weathers All Storms (9") 912883	P. Hillman	OP	160.00	160.00
1993-43-067	Theordore, Smantha & Tyler "Friendship Weathers All Storms" (Musical) 904546	P. Hillman	OP	170.00	170.00
1993-43-068	Mary "A Special Friend Warms The Season" 912840	P. Hillman	OP	25.00	25.00
1993-43-069	"Friends Like You Are Precious And True" 904309	P. Hillman	OP	30.00	30.00
1993-43-070	"Friendship Pulls Us Through" & "Ewe Make Being Friends Special" 912867	P. Hillman	OP	13.50	13.50
1993-43-071	"Cherish The King" (Musical) 912859	P. Hillman	OP	60.00	60.00
1993-43-072	Gretel "We Make Magic, Me And You" 912778	P. Hillman	OP	18.50	18.50
1993-43-073	Gary "True Friendships Are Scarce" 912778	P. Hillman	OP	18.50	18.50
1993-43-074	Connie "You're A Sweet Treat" 912794	P. Hillman	OP	15.00	15.00
1993-43-075	Miles "I'm Thankful For A Friend Like You" 912751	P. Hillman	OP	17.00	17.00
1993-43-076	Prudence "A Friend To Be Thankful For" 912808	P. Hillman	OP	17.00	17.00
1993-43-077	Bucky & Brenda "How I Love Being Friends With You" 912816	P. Hillman	OP	15.00	15.00
1994-43-078	Victoria "From My Heart To Yours" 916293	P. Hillman	SUSP	16.50	45-65.00
1994-43-079	Nancy "Your Friendship Makes My Heart Sing" 916315	P. Hillman	OP	15.00	15.00
1994-43-080	Kelly "You're My One And Only" 916307	P. Hillman	OP	15.00	15.00
1994-43-081	Oliver & Olivia "Will You Be Mine?" 916641	P. Hillman	OP	25.00	25.00
1994-43-082	Elizabeth & Ashley "My Beary Best Friend" 916277	P. Hillman	OP	25.00	25.00
1994-43-083	"Friendship Is Love That Lasts" (Musical) 916323	P. Hillman	OP	45.00	45.00
1994-43-084	Kathleen "Luck Found Me A Friend In You" 916447	P. Hillman	OP	12.50	12.50
1994-43-085	Sean "Luck Found Me A Friend In You" 916439	P. Hillman	OP	12.50	12.50
1994-43-086	"Some Bunny Loves You" (Musical) 625302	P. Hillman	OP	60.00	60.00
1994-43-087	Becky "Springtime Happiness" 916331	P. Hillman	OP	20.00	20.00
1994-43-088	Faith "There's No Bunny Like You" 916412	P. Hillman	SUSP	20.00	55.00
1994-43-089	Henry "Celebrating Spring With You" 916420	P. Hillman	SUSP	20.00	40.00
1994-43-090	Bessie "Some Bunny Loves You" 916404	P. Hillman	SUSP	15.00	40-60.00
1994-43-091	Courtney "Springtime Is A Blessing From Above" 916390	P. Hillman	OP	15.00	15.00
1994-43-092	"A Mother's Love Bears All Things" 624861	P. Hillman	OP	20.00	20.00
1994-43-093	"A Father Is The Bearer Of Strength" 624888	P. Hillman	OP	13.50	13.50
1994-43-094	Older Daughter "Child Of Love" 624845	P. Hillman	OP	10.00	10.00
1994-43-095	Older Son "Child Of Pride" 624829	P. Hillman	OP	10.00	10.00
1994-44-096	Young Daughter "Child Of Kindness" 624853	P. Hillman	OP	9.00	9.00
1994-43-097	Young Son "Child Of Hope" 624837	P. Hillman	OP	9.00	9.00
1994-43-098	Jack & Jill "Our Friendship Will Never Tumble" 624772	P. Hillman	OP	30.00	30.00
1994-43-099	Mary, Mary Quite Contrary "Friendship Blooms With Loving Care" 626074	P. Hillman	OP	22.50	22.50
1994-43-100	Tom, Tom The Piper's Son "Wherever You Go I'll Follow" 624810	P. Hillman	OP	20.00	20.00

RELEASE YEAR	FIGURINE	ARTIST	EDITION	ISSUE	QUOTE
1994-43-101	Little Jack Horner "I'm Plum Happy You're My Friend" 624780	P. Hillman	OP	20.00	20.00
1994-43-102	Little Miss Muffet "I'm Never Afraid With You At My Side" 624799	P. Hillman	OP	20.00	20.00
1994-43-103	Little Bo Peep "Looking For A Friend Like You" 624802	P. Hillman	OP	22.50	22.50
1994-43-104	"Cuddle Me With Love" (Musical) 699322	P. Hillman	OP	60.00	60.00
1994-43-105	"A Playful Friend" (Musical) 699314	P. Hillman	OP	60.00	60.00
1994-43-106	Betty "Bubblin' Over With Love" 626066	P. Hillman	OP	18.50	18.50
1994-43-107	Billy "Everyone Needs A Cuddle' Betsey "First Step To Love" Bobby "A Little Friendship To Share" 624896	P. Hillman	OP	12.50	12.50
1994-43-108	Robbie & Rachel "Love Bears All Things" (Musical) 699349	P. Hillman	OP	50.00	50.00
1994-43-109	Christopher "Old Friends Are The Best Friends" (Musical) 627453	P. Hillman	OP	60.00	60.00
1994-43-110	Katie "A Friend Always Knows When You Need a Hug" (Musical) 627445	P. Hillman	OP	45.00	45.00
1994-43-111	Nursery Rhyme Books CRTO13	P. Hillman	OP	40.00	40.00
1994-43-112	"My Favorite Things - A Cuddle And You" 628565	P. Hillman	OP	150.00	150.00
1994-43-113	"Smooth Sailing" (Musical) 624926	P. Hillman	OP	60.00	60.00
1994-43-114	Taylor "Sail The Seas With Me" 617156	P. Hillman	OP	15.00	15.00
1994-43-115	Breanna "Pumpkin Patch Pals" 617180	P. Hillman	OP	15.00	15.00
1994-43-116	Stacie "You Lift My Spirit" 617148	P. Hillman	OP	18.50	18.50
1994-43-117	Patience "Happiness Is Homemade" 617105	P. Hillman	OP	17.50	17.50
1994-43-118	Wyatt "I'm Called Little Running Bear" 629707	P. Hillman	OP	15.00	15.00
1994-43-119	Jedediah "Giving Thanks For Friends" 617091	P. Hillman	OP	17.50	17.50
1994-43-120	Thanksgiving Quilt 617075	P. Hillman	OP	12.10	12.00
1994-43-121	Phoebe "A Little Friendship Is A Big Blessing" 617113	P. Hillman	OP	13.50	13.50
1994-43-122	Wylie "I'm Called LIttle Friend" 617121	P. Hillman	OP	15.00	15.00
1994-43-123	Winona "Fair Feather Friends" 617172	P. Hillman	OP	15.00	15.00
1994-43-124	Willie "Bears Of A Feather Stay Together" 617164	P. Hillman	OP	15.00	15.00
1994-43-125	Gloria "Ghost of Christmas Past" Garland "Ghost Of Christmas Present" Gabriel "Ghost of Christmas Yet To Come" 614807	P. Hillman	OP	55.00	55.00
1994-43-126	Mrs. Cratchit "A Beary Christmas And Happy New Year!" 617318	P. Hillman	OP	18.50	18.50
1994-43-127	Tiny Ted-bear "God Bless Us Everyone" 614777	P. Hillman	OP	10.00	10.00
1994-43-128	Jacob Bearly "You Will Be Haunted By Three Spirits" 614785	P. Hillman	OP	17.50	17.50
1994-43-129	Bear Cratchit "And A Very Merry Christmas To You Mr. Scrooge" 617326	P. Hillman	OP	17.50	17.50
1994-43-130	Ebearneezer Scrooge "Bah Humbug!" 617296	P. Hillman	OP	17.50	17.50
1994-43-131	Cratchit's House 651362	P. Hillman	OP	75.00	75.00
1994-43-132	Counting House 622788	P. Hillman	OP	75.00	75.00
1994-43-133	Sonja 'Holiday Cuddles" 622818	P. Hillman	OP	20.00	20.00
1994-43-134	Nils "Near And Deer For Christmas" 617245	P. Hillman	OP	22.50	22.50
1994-43-135	Eric "Bear Tidings Of Joy" 622796	P. Hillman	OP	22.50	22.50
1994-43-136	Ingrid"Bundled Up With Warm Wishes" Dated 1994 - 617237	P. Hillman	Yr.Iss.	20.00	40.00
1994-43-137	"Tis The Season For Deer Friends" (Musical) 629618	P. Hillman	OP	165.00	165.00
1994-43-138	"Bundled Up For The Holidays" (Musical) 651435	P. Hillman	OP	100.00	100.00
1994-43-139	"That's What Friends Are For" 651095	P. Hillman	OP	22.50	22.50
1994-43-143	Ronnie "I'll Play My Drum For You" 912905	P. Hillman	OP	13.50	13.50
1995-43-144	Earl "Warm Hearted Friends" 131873	P. Hillman	OP	17.50	17.50
1995-43-145	Tucker & Travis "We're In This Together" 127973	P. Hillman	OP	25.00	25.00
1995-43-146	Seth & Sarabeth "We're Beary Good Pals" 128015	P. Hillman	OP	25.00	25.00
1995-43-147	The Best Is Yet To Come 127957	P. Hillman	OP	12.50	12.50
1995-43-148	Priscilla & Greta "Our Hearts Belong To You" 128031	P. Hillman	LD19,950	50.00	50.00
1995-43-149	Kiss The Hurt And Make It Well 127965	P. Hillman	OP	15.00	15.00
1995-43-150	Allison & Alexandria "Two Friends Mean Twice The Love" 127981	P. Hillman	OP	25.00	25.00

Release Year	Figurine	Artist	Edition	Issue	Quote
1995-43-151	Dorothy, Millie, Christy 128023	P. Hillman	OP	12.50	12.50
1995-43-152	Madeline "A Cup Full of Cheer" 135593 Margaret "A Cup Full Of Love" 135682 Marilyn "A Cup Full of Friendship" 135682	P. Hillman	OP	20.00	20.00
1995-43-153	Christine "My Prayer Is For You" 103845	P. Hillman	OP	18.50	18.50
1995-43-154	Christian "My Prayer Is For You" 103837	P. Hillman	OP	18.50	18.50
1995-43-155	"AuClaire De Lune" (Musical) 128058	P. Hillman	OP	55.00	55.00
1995-43-156	Carrie "The Future Beareth All Things" 141321	P. Hillman	OP	18.50	18.50
1995-43-157	Bea "Bee My Friend" 141348	P. Hillman	OP	15.00	15.00
1995-43-158	Pat "Falling For You" 141313	P. Hillman	OP	22.50	22.50
1995-43-159	"Yule Building A Sturdy Friendship" 141143	P. Hillman	OP	22.50	22.50
1995-43-160	"Ginger Painting Your Holidays With Love" 141127	P. Hillman	OP	22.50	22.50
1995-43-161	Meri "Handsewn Holidays" 141135	P. Hillman	OP	20.00	20.00
1995-43-162	Nickolas "You're At The Top Of My List" 141100	P. Hillman	OP	20.00	20.00
1995-43-163	Holly "A Cup of Homemade Love" 141119	P. Hillman	OP	18.50	18.50
1995-43-164	Amanda "Here's Some Cheer To Last The Year" 141186	P. Hillman	Yr.Iss.	17.50	25.00
1995-43-165	Kristen "Hugs Of Love And Friendship" 141194	P. Hillman	OP	20.00	20.00
1995-43-166	Celeste "An Angel To Watch" 141267	P. Hillman	OP	20.00	20.00
1995-43-167	Jack "A New Year With Old Friends" 914754	P. Hillman	OP	15.00	15.00
1995-43-168	Phoebe "Be Mine" 914762	P. Hillman	OP	15.00	15.00
1995-43-169	Mark "Friendship Is In The Air" 914770	P. Hillman	OP	15.00	15.00
1995-43-170	Alan "Showers Of Friendship" 914789	P. Hillman	OP	15.00	15.00
1995-43-171	Nichole "Thanks For Friends" 914851	P. Hillman	OP	15.00	15.00
1995-43-172	Denise "Happy Holidays, Friends" 914878	P. Hillman	OP	15.00	15.00
1995-43-173	May "Friendship Is In Bloom" 914797	P. Hillman	OP	15.00	15.00
1995-43-174	June "Planting The Seed Of Friendship" 914800	P. Hillman	OP	15.00	15.00
1995-43-175	Julie "A Day In The Park" 914819	P. Hillman	OP	15.00	15.00
1995-43-176	Arthur "Smooth Sailing" 914827	P. Hillman	OP	15.00	15.00
1995-43-177	Seth "School Days" 914835	P. Hillman	OP	15.00	15.00
1995-43-178	Oscar "Sweet Treats" 914843	P. Hillman	OP	15.00	15.00

Enesco® Corporation – SPECIAL LIMITED CHERISHED TEDDIES®

Release Year	Figurine	Artist	Edition	Issue	Quote
1993-44-001	Teddy & Roosevelt "The Book Of Teddies 1903-1993" 624918	P. Hillman	Yr.Iss.	20.00	75.00
1993-44-002	Holding On To Someone Special Collector Appreciation Figurine 916285	P. Hillman	Yr.Iss.	20.00	60.00
1993-44-003	Priscilla Ann "There's No One Like Hue" Collectible Exposition Exclusive available only at Secaucus and South Bend in 1994 and at Long Beach in 1995	P. Hillman	Yr.Iss.	24.00	65.00

Enesco® Corporation – CHERISHED TEDDIES® CLUB

Release Year	Figurine	Artist	Edition	Issue	Quote
1995-45-001	Cub E. Bear CT001	P. Hillman	Yr.Iss.	Gift	25.00
1995-45-002	Mayor Wilson T. Beary CT951	P. Hillman	Yr.Iss.	20.00	20.00
1995-45-003	Hilary Hugabear C952	P. Hillman	Yr.Iss.	17.50	17.50

Enesco® Corporation – LUCY AND ME® COLLECTION

Release Year	Figurine	Artist	Edition	Issue	Quote
1979-01-101	4 Bears With Red Bows E3125	L. Rigg	RT 1989	8-12.00	20.00
1979-01-102	4 Bears With Shirts On E3128	L. Rigg	RT 1989	8-12.00	20.00
1979-01-103	2 Couples With Red Bows E3197	L. Rigg	RT 1986	8-12.00	20.00
1979-01-104	2 Bears With Indoor Plants E4727	L. Rigg	RT 1985	8-12.00	20.00
1979-01-105	Bride And Groom E4728	L. Rigg	OP	8-12.00	8-12.00
1979-01-106	2 Bears In Bunny Ears E4731	L. Rigg	RT 1985	8-12.00	20.00
1979-01-107	2 Bears With Birthday Props E4732	L. Rigg	RT 1986	8-12.00	20.00
1979-01-108	2 Moms Hugging Cubs E4733	L. Rigg	RT 1988	8-12.00	20.00
1979-01-109	Doctor And Nurse E4735	L. Rigg	RT 1990	8-12.00	20.00
1979-01-110	World's Greatest Dad E4736	L. Rigg	RT 1986	8-12.00	20.00
1979-01-111	Bear In Irish Suit E4737	L. Rigg	RT 1985	8-12.00	20.00
1979-01-112	Football, Basketball, Baseball, Soccer E4739	L. Rigg	OP	8-12.00	20.00
1979-01-113	2 Carolers With Cats and "Joy To The World" Books E2814	L. Rigg	RT 1982	8-12.00	20.00

RELEASE YEAR	FIGURINE	ARTIST	EDITION	ISSUE	QUOTE
1989-01-515	Gnome Smoking/Gnome Skiing 222062	L. Rigg	RT 1990	10.00	15.00
1989-01-516	Nativity Bunny, Goose, Dove, Chicken 222070	L. Rigg	RT 1990	10.00	15.00
1989-01-517	Nativity Bear On Camel 222089	L. Rigg	RT 1990	10.00	15.00
1989-01-518	"A Christmas Carol" Scrooge Dated 1989 222100	L. Rigg	Yr.Iss. 1989	10.00	15.00
1990-01-519	"1990" Boy With Candy And Rose 223743	L. Rigg	Yr.Iss. 1990	10.00	15.00
1990-01-520	Bat, Superman, Devil 228168	L. Rigg	RT 1993	10.00	15.00
1990-01-521	Bear Dressed As Cornacopia 228176	L. Rigg	OP	10.00	10.00
1990-01-522	Girl/Boy Cavebears 228184	L. Rigg	RT 1993	10.00	15.00
1990-01-523	Cowgirl/Cowboy 228192	L. Rigg	RT 1993	10.00	15.00
1990-01-524	Indian Boy/ Indian Girl 228206	L. Rigg	OP	10.00	10.00
1990-01-525	Girl/Boy Tennis Players 229040	L. Rigg	RT 1993	10.00	15.00
1990-01-526	Fireman 229075	L. Rigg	OP	10.00	10.00
1990-01-527	Bear Dressed As Ice Cream Cone 229083	L. Rigg	RT 1993	10.00	15.00
1990-01-528	Butler/Maid 229091	L. Rigg	RT 1993	10.00	15.00
1990-01-529	Mail Carrier 229113	L. Rigg	OP	10.00	10.00
1990-01-530	Noah's Ark Lion 229121	L. Rigg	OP	10.00	10.00
1990-01-531	Bear Dressed As Trick-or-Treat Bag 229547	L. Rigg	OP	10.00	10.00
1990-01-532	Bear Dressed As Easter Basket 229857	L. Rigg	OP	10.00	10.00
1990-01-533	Radish, Seed Packet, Barrel of Vegetables 299865	L. Rigg	RT 1993	10.00	15.00
1990-01-534	Ladybug/Honey Bee 229873	L. Rigg	OP	10.00	10.00
1990-01-535	Bear Dressed As A Chick 229881	L. Rigg	RT 1993	10.00	15.00
1990-01-536	Girl Dressed In Easter Clothes 229003	L. Rigg	RT 1992	10.00	15.00
1990-01-537	3 Bears In Diapers And Bunny Ears 229911	L. Rigg	OP	10.00	10.00
1990-01-538	Bear Dressed As Fortune Cookie 230936	L. Rigg	RT 1992	10.00	15.00
1990-01-539	Bear Dressed As Chinese Take-Out 230944	L. Rigg	OP	10.00	10.00
1990-01-540	Bear Dressed As A Taco 230952	L. Rigg	RT 1993	10.00	15.00
1990-01-541	Bear Dressed As A Donkey 230960	L. Rigg	RT 1992	10.00	15.00
1990-01-542	Bear Dressed As A Sheep 230979	L. Rigg	RT 1992	10.00	15.00
1990-01-543	Noah 230987	L. Rigg	OP	10.00	10.00
1990-01-544	Noah's Wife 230995	L.. Rigg	OP	10.00	10.00
1990-01-545	Noah's Ark Elephant 231002	L. Rigg	OP	10.00	10.00
1990-01-546	Noah's Ark Monkey 231010	L. Rigg	OP	10.00	10.00
1990-01-547	Noah's Ark Zebra 231029	L. Rigg	OP	10.00	10.00
1990-01-548	Noah's Ark Tiger 231037	L. Rigg	OP	10.00	10.00
1990-01-549	Noah's Ark Turtle 231045	L. Rigg	RT 1993	10.00	15.00
1990-01-550	Noah's Ark Giraffe 231053	L. Rigg	OP	10.00	10.00
1990-01-551	Noah's Ark Toucan 231061	L. Rigg	OP	10.00	10.00
1990-01-552	Sweet Sixteen Girl 513202	L. Rigg	RT 1992	10.00	15.00
1990-01-553	Wicked Witch Of The West 513210	L. Rigg	RT 1993	10.00	15.00
1990-01-554	Soccer Player 513229	L. Rigg	RT 1993	10.00	15.00
1990-01-555	Basketball Player #23 513237	L. Rigg	RT. 1993	10.00	15.00
1990-01-556	Marilyn Monroe 513245	L. Rigg	RT 1993	10.00	15.00
1990-01-557	Captain Hook 513253	L. Rigg	RT 1993	10.00	15.00
1990-01-558	Peter Pan 513261	L. Rigg	RT 1993	10.00	15.00
1990-01-559	Wendy 513288	L. Rigg	RT 1993	10.00	15.00
1990-01-560	Tinkerbell 513296	L. Rigg	RT 1993	10.00	15.00
1990-01-561	Crocodile With Clock 513318	L. Rigg	RT 1993	10.00	15.00
1990-01-562	Mermaid 513326	L. Rigg	RT 1993	10.00	15.00
1990-01-563	Tom Tom The Piper's Son 513334	L. Rigg	RT 1992	10.00	15.00
1990-01-564	Little Bo Peep 513342	L. Rigg	RT 1993	10.00	15.00
1990-01-565	Bear Dressed As Mushroom 513377	L. Rigg	RT 1992	10.00	15.00
1990-01-566	Bear Dressed As Green Pepper 513385	L. Rigg	RT 1992	10.00	15.00
1990-01-567	Elvis Presley 513393	L. Rigg	OP	10.00	10.00
1990-01-568	Mary Poppins 513407	L. Rigg	RT 1992	10.00	15.00
1990-01-569	Pilgrim Boy/Girl 513741	L. Rigg	OP	10.00	10.00
1990-01-570	3 Tumbling Gnomes 22714	L. Rigg	OP	10.00	
1990-01-571	3 Bears Dressed As Ball Ornaments 228095	L. Rigg	RT 1993	10.00	15.00
1990-01-572	"1990" Bear Dressed As Holly Wreath 228117	L. Rigg	Yr.Iss 1990	10.00	15.00
1990-01-573	Bear Holding Miltletoe 228133	L. Rigg	OP	10.00	10.00
1990-01-574	2 Cross-Country Skiers 228141	L. Rigg	OP	10.00	10.00
1990-01-575	3 Elves Building 3 Toys 228214	L. Rigg	OP	10.00	10.00
1990-01-576	Gnome Carrying Gifts 228249	L. Rigg	OP	10.00	10.00
1990-01-577	Bear Dressed As Jingle Bell 513121	L. Rigg	OP	10.00	10.00
1990-01-578	Girl/Boy Skier With Broken Legs 513553	L. Rigg	OP	10.00	10.00
1990-01-579	Girl/Goy Skaters 513636	L. Rigg	OP	10.00	10.00
1991-01-580	Pencil For Teacher 232475	L. Rigg	OP	10.00	10.00
1991-01-581	Three Crayons: Red, Yellow, Blue 232483	L. Rigg	RT 1993	10.00	15.00
1991-01-582	Maple Leaf, Oak Leaf, Hazelnut 234567	L. Rigg	OP	10.00	10.00
1991-01-583	Pizza 235814	L. Rigg	OP	10.00	10.00

147

RELEASE YEAR	FIGURINE	ARTIST	EDITION	ISSUE	QUOTE
1991-01-584	Submarine Sandwich 235822	L. Rigg	OP	10.00	10.00
1991-01-585	Noah's Ark Kangaroo 235830	L. Rigg	RT 1993	10.00	15.00
1991-01-586	Owl 235849	L. Rigg	RT 1993	10.00	15.00
1991-01-587	Frog 235857	L. Rigg	RT 1993	10.00	15.00
1991-01-588	Red Hot Chili Pepper 235873	L. Rigg	RT 1993	10.00	15.00
1991-01-589	Phantom Of The Opera 235903	L. Rigg	OP	10.00	10.00
1991-01-590	Lone Ranger 235911	L. Rigg	OP	10.00	10.00
1991-01-591	Tonto 235938	L. Rigg	OP	10.00	10.00
1991-01-592	Bowling Pin 235954	L. Rigg	OP	10.00	10.00
1991-01-593	Grapes 235962	L. Rigg	RT 1993	10.00	15.00
1991-01-594	Lemon 235970	L. Rigg	RT 1993	10.00	15.00
1991-01-595	Army 235989	L. Rigg	RT 1993	10.00	15.00
1991-01-596	Navy 235997	L. Rigg	RT 1993	10.00	15.00
1991-01-597	Air Force 236004	L. Rigg	RT 1993	10.00	15.00
1991-01-598	Marine 236012	L. Rigg	RT 1993	10.00	15.00
1991-01-599	Lucy As An Animal Lover 236020	L. Rigg	OP	10.00	10.00
1991-01-600	Christopher Columbus 236144	L. Rigg	RT 1992	10.00	15.00
1991-01-601	Lily And Pansy 236179	L. Rigg	OP	10.00	10.00
1991-01-602	Buttlerfly 236160	L. Rigg	OP	10.00	10.00
1991-01-603	3 Easter Eggs 236187	L. Rigg	RT 1993	10.00	15.00
1991-01-604	Robin 236195	L. Rigg	RT 1993	10.00	15.00
1991-01-605	Snail And Caterpillar 236209	L. Rigg	OP	10.00	10.00
1991-01-606	Bear Dressed As Kite 236217	L. Rigg	RT 1993	10.00	15.00
1991-01-607	Bear Dressed As Sun/Rainbow 236225	L. Rigg	RT 1993	10.00	15.00
1991-01-608	Bear Dressed As A Skunk 236306	L. Rigg	RT 1993	10.00	15.00
1991-01-609	Candy Heart 236896	L. Rigg	RT 1993	10.00	15.00
1991-01-610	Hansel And Gretel 237809	L. Rigg	RT 1993	10.00	15.00
1991-01-611	Pineappple 239224	L. Rigg	RT 1993	10.00	15.00
1991-01-612	Bear Dressed As Clam, Bear Dressed As Lobster 239232	L. Rigg	OP	10.00	10.00
1991-01-613	Lucy And Me Collector's Sign 239240	L. Rigg	OP	10.00	10.00
1991-01-614	Watermelon 239259	L. Rigg	OP	10.00	10.00
1991-01-615	Bear Dressed As Holly Bush 234583	L. Rigg	OP	10.00	10.00
1991-01-616	Bear Dressed As Pinecone 234591	L. Rigg	OP	10.00	10.00
1991-01-617	2 Bears Dressed As Cookie 234613	L. Rigg	OP	10.00	10.00
1991-01-618	Elf Holding Gingerbread Cookie 234621	L. Rigg	OP	10.00	10.00
1991-01-619	"1991" Bear Dressed As Peppermint Candy 236659	L. Rigg	Yr.Iss. 1991	10.00	25.00
1992-01-620	Lucy Birthday Parade, Age 4 233919	L. Rigg	OP	10.00	15.00
1992-01-621	Baby In Christening Gown 233994	L. Rigg	OP	10.00	10.00
1992-01-622	Baby Boy Eating Out Of Bowl 234001	L. Rigg	RT 1993	7.50	15.00
1992-01-623	Baby Girl Drinking From Mug 234028	L. Rigg	RT 1993	7.50	15.00
1992-01-624	Valentine's Day Card 236292	L. Rigg	OP	10.00	10.00
1992-01-625	2 Bears Dressed As Pumpkins 242888	L. Rigg	OP	10.00	10.00
1992-01-626	Halloween Costume 243078	L. Rigg	OP	10.00	10.00
1992-01-627	Daffodil And Daisy In Pot 243442	L. Rigg	OP	10.00	10.00
1992-01-628	Chocolate Candy 246344	L. Rigg	OP	10.00	10.00
1992-01-629	Ice Cream Soda 246352	L. Rigg	OP	10.00	10.00
1992-01-630	Dalmatian (Dottie) 246360	L. Rigg	OP	10.00	10.00
1992-01-631	Ice Cream Sundae 246395	L. Rigg	OP	10.00	10.00
1992-01-632	Berry Bears 246409	L. Rigg	OP	10.00	10.00
1992-01-633	Bluebird 246751	L. Rigg	OP	10.00	10.00
1992-01-634	Bear With Conversation Hearts 246778	L. Rigg	OP	10.00	10.00
1992-01-635	Tricerotops Dinosaur 247677	L. Rigg	OP	10.00	10.00
1992-01-636	Tropical Fish 247685	L. Rigg	OP	10.00	10.00
1992-01-637	Dolphin 247693	L. Rigg	OP	10.00	10.00
1992-01-638	Harpo 247707	L. Rigg	OP	10.00	10.00
1992-01-639	Groucho 247723	L. Rigg	OP	10.00	10.00
1992-01-640	Bible Classics - Eve 247731	L. Rigg	OP	10.00	10.00
1992-01-641	Bible Classics - Adam 247758	L. Rigg	OP	10.00	10.00
1992-01-642	Noah's Ark - Beaver 247766	L. Rigg	OP	10.00	10.00
1992-01-643	Noah's Ark - Moose 247774	L. Rigg	OP	10.00	10.00
1992-01-644	Noah's Ark - Penguin 247782	L. Rigg	OP	10.00	10.00
1992-01-645	Stegosquraus 247790	L. Rigg	OP	10.00	10.00
1992-01-646	Tyrannosaurus 247804	L. Rigg	OP	10.00	10.00
1992-01-647	Chocolate Cookie 24781	L. Rigg	OP	10.00	10.00
1992-01-648	Carton Of Milk 247820	L. Rigg	OP	10.00	10.00
1992-01-649	Nurse 247839	L. Rigg	OP	10.00	10.00
1992-01-650	Nun 247847	L. Rigg	OP	10.00	10.00
1992-01-651	Priest 247855	L. Rigg	OP˙	10.00	10.00
1992-01-652	Bear Holding Toothbrush 247863	L. Rigg	OP	10.00	10.00

Release Year	Figurine	Artist	Edition	Issue	Quote
1992-01-653	Bear Dressed As Toothpaste 247871	L. Rigg	OP	10.00	10.00
1992-01-654	Hot Water Bottle 247901	L. Rigg	OP	10.00	10.00
1992-01-655	"Take A Hike" Walker 247936	L. Rigg	OP	10.00	10.00
1992-01-656	Birthday Parade, Age 1 247952	L. Rigg	OP	10.00	10.00
1992-01-657	Birthday Parade, Age 2 247979	L. Rigg	OP	10.00	10.00
1992-01-658	Birthday Parade, Age 3 247987	L. Rigg	OP	10.00	10.00
1992-01-659	Birthday Parade, Age 5 247995	L. Rigg	OP	10.00	10.00
1992-01-660	Birthday Parade, Age 6 248002	L. Rigg	OP	10.00	10.00
1992-01-661	50's Girl With Bells 232934	L. Rigg	OP	10.00	10.00
1992-01-662	Bear Wrapped In Lights 242942	L. Rigg	OP	10.00	10.00
1992-01-663	Bear Dressed As Bells 242950	L. Rigg	OP	10.00	10.00
1992-01-664	Bear Dressed As Globe 243094	L. Rigg	OP	10.00	10.00
1992-01-665	Event Blue Ribbon 237817	L. Rigg	LD 1500	10.00	20.00
1992-01-666	Santa Coming To Town 243108	L. Rigg	OP	10.00	10.00
1992-01-667	2 Bears Dressed As Toys: Ragdoll Drummer 243116	L. Rigg	OP	10.00	10.00
1992-01-668	Drum/Block 243124	L. Rigg	OP	10.00	10.00
1992-01-669	3 Nativity Angels 243132	L. Rigg	OP	10.00	10.00
1992-01-670	"1992" Dated Caroler 243140	L. Rigg	Yr.Iss. 1992	10.00	20.00
1992-01-671	Bears Dressed As Christmas Cookies 243159	L. Rigg	OP	10.00	10.00
1993-01-672	Dressed As Vegetable Crates 244635	L. Rigg	OP	10.00	10.00
1993-01-673	Banana Split 246379	L. Rigg	OP	10.00	10.00
1993-01-674	Dracula And Elvira 250074	L. Rigg	OP	10.00	10.00
1993-01-675	Halloween Fairy Princess & Clown 250082	L. Rigg	OP	10.00	10.00
1993-01-676	Halloween Cat, Hobo, Gypsy 250104	L. Rigg	OP	10.00	10.00
1993-01-677	5 Piece Thanksgiving Set 251186	L. Rigg	OP	10.00	10.00
1993-01-678	Loving Cup 15th Anniversary Piece 251348	L. Rigg	Yr.Iss. 1993	10.00	20.00
1993-01-679	Bell Ringer 250066	L. Rigg	OP	10.00	10.00
1993-01-680	Eskimo 250090	L. Rigg	OP	10.00	10.00
1993-01-681	2 Bears Dressed As Cookies 250171	L. Rigg	OP	10.00	10.00
1993-01-682	Dad With Lights 250198	L. Rigg	OP	10.00	10.00
1993-01-683	"1993" Snowflalke 250228	L. Rigg	Yr.Iss. 1993	10.00	15.00
1993-01-684	3 Angels With Instruments 250236	L. Rigg	OP	10.00	10.00
1993-01-685	Girl With Creche 250244	L. Rigg	OP	10.00	10.00
1993-01-686	Boy With Train 250260	L. Rigg	OP	10.00	10.00
1993-01-687	Mom With Cranberries 250279	L. Rigg	OP	10.00	10.00
1993-01-688	Toy Top 250309	L. Rigg	OP	10.00	10.00
1994-01-689	Event Gold Metal Piece (1994) 206396	L. Rigg	Yr.Iss. 1994	10.00	20.00
1994-01-690	Uncle Sam 244732	L. Rigg	OP	10.00	10.00
1994-01-691	Lucy As Birth Certificate 244740	L. Rigg	OP	10.00	10.00
1994-01-692	3 Baby Bottles 244759	L. Rigg	OP	10.00	10.00
1994-01-693	Ring Toy 244767	L. Rigg	OP	10.00	10.00
1994-01-694	Policeman 244775	L. Rigg	OP	10.00	10.00
1994-01-695	Doctor In Scrubs 244783	L. Rigg	OP	10.00	10.00
1994-01-696	Beautician 244791	L. Rigg	OP	10.00	10.00
1994-01-697	Ice Cream Sandwich 247278	L. Rigg	OP	10.00	10.00
1994-01-698	Cup Cake 247286	L. Rigg	OP	10.00	10.00
1994-01-699	Slice Of Cake 247294	L. Rigg	OP	10.00	10.00
1994-01-700	Construction Worker 249513	L. Rigg	OP	10.00	10.00
1994-01-701	Fishing Creel 249556	L. Rigg	OP	10.00	10.00
1994-01-702	Picnic Basket 249580	L. Rigg	OP	10.00	10.00
1994-01-703	Jar Of Baby Food 249920	L. Rigg	OP	10.00	10.00
1994-01-704	Teacher 249939	L. Rigg	OP	10.00	10.00
1994-01-705	Chocolate Bunny 255602	L. Rigg	OP	10.00	10.00
1994-01-706	3 Chocolate Eggs 255610	L. Rigg	OP	10.00	10.00
1994-01-707	3 Bunny Bears Sitting In Baskets 255629	L. Rigg	OP	10.00	10.00
1994-01-708	Bunny Bear 255637	L. Rigg	OP	10.00	10.00
1994-01-709	3 Baby Bears Dressed As Bunnies 255645	L. Rigg	OP	10.00	10.00
1994-01-710	Strawberry Shortcake 255726	L. Rigg	OP	10.00	10.00
1994-01-711	Watering Can 255734	L. Rigg	OP	10.00	10.00
1994-01-712	Birdhouse 255742	L. Rigg	OP	10.00	10.00
1994-01-713	Envelope 255785	L. Rigg	OP	10.00	10.00
1994-01-714	Mailbox 255793	L. Rigg	OP	10.00	10.00
1994-01-715	3 Cupid Bears Sitting/Standing/Sleeping 255807	L. Rigg	OP	10.00	10.00
1994-01-716	3 Angels With Nativity 206342	L. Rigg	OP	10.00	10.00
1994-01-717	Bear Dressed As Teddy 206377	L. Rigg	OP	10.00	10.00
1994-01-718	Mrs. Claus 206407	L. Rigg	OP	10.00	10.00
1994-01-719	Blitzen 206474	L. Rigg	OP	10.00	10.00
1994-01-720	Dancer 206490	L. Rigg	OP	10.00	10.00
1994-01-721	Prancer 206482	L. Rigg	OP	10.00	10.00
1994-01-722	Vixen 206458	L. Rigg	OP	10.00	10.00

ENESCO® CORPORATION – LUCY AND ME® COLLECTION

RELEASE YEAR	FIGURINE	ARTIST	EDITION	ISSUE	QUOTE
1994-01-723	Cupid 206423	L. Rigg	OP	10.00	10.00
1994-01-724	Donner 206415	L. Rigg	OP	10.00	10.00
1994-01-725	Dasher 206431	L. Rigg	OP	10.00	10.00
1994-01-726	Comet 20646	L. Rigg	OP	10.00	10.00
1994-01-727	Elf Holding North Pole Sign 206504	L. Rigg	OP	10.00	10.00
1994-01-728	Bear Dressed As Wrapped Present 206520	L. Rigg	OP	10.00	10.00
1994-01-729	Bear Dressed As Spool Of Ribbon 206539	L. Rigg	OP	10.00	10.00
1994-01-730	Bear Dressed As Wrapping Paper 206547	L. Rigg	OP	10.00	10.00
1994-01-731	Jack-In-The-Box 206563	L. Rigg	OP	10.00	10.00
1994-01-732	Santa Claus With Toys 252999	L. Rigg	OP	10.00	10.00
1995-01-733	Lucy & Me Limited Edition 127698	L. Rigg	LD 2000	30.00	35.00
1995-01-734	Bear Holding 1st Place Ribbon 127523	L. Rigg	OP	10.00	10.00
1995-01-735	Bear Dressed As Dice 127558	L. Rigg	OP	10.00	10.00
1995-01-736	Bear Dressed As Vase Of Roses 127574	L. Rigg	OP	10.00	10.00
1995-01-737	Bear Holding Birthday Cake 127582	L. Rigg	OP	10.00	10.00
1995-01-738	Bear Holding Report Card 127590	L. Rigg	OP	10.00	10.00
1995-01-739	Bear As Ballerina 127604	L. Rigg	OP	10.00	10.00
1995-01-740	Bear Dressed As Trophy 127612	L. Rigg	OP	10.00	10.00
1995-01-741	Bear Dressed As Bride 127620	L. Rigg	OP	10.00	10.00
1995-01-742	Boy Square Dancer 127671	L. Rigg	OP	10.00	10.00
1995-01-743	Girl Square Dancer 127663	L. Rigg	OP	10.00	10.00
1995-01-744	Bear Holding BINGO Card 127655	L. Rigg	OP	10.00	10.00
1995-01-745	Statue Of Liberty 136530	L. Rigg	OP	10.00	10.00
1995-01-746	Uncle Sam 244732	L. Rigg	OP	10.00	10.00
1995-01-747	World Greatest Secretary 127639	L. Rigg	OP	10.00	10.00
1995-01-748	Kiss The Cook 127657	L. Rigg	OP	10.00	10.00

ENESCO® CORPORATION – CHAPEAU NOELLE™ COLLECTION

RELEASE YEAR	FIGURINE	ARTIST	EDITION	ISSUE	QUOTE
1994-01-001	"Joan" With Hand Mirror	L. Rigg	LD 2000/CL	30.00	45.00
1994-01-002	"Linda" With Tea Cup	L. Rigg	LD 2000/CL	30.00	45.00
1994-01-003	"Diane" Bride	L. Rigg	LD 2000/CL	30.00	45.00
1994-01-004	Romeo	L. Rigg	LD 2000	30.00	45.00
1994-01-005	Juliet	L. Rigg	LD 2000	30.00	45.00
1994-01-006	Susie	L. Rigg	LD 2000	30.00	45.00
1994-01-007	Allison	L. Rigg	LD 2000	30.00	45.00
1994-01-008	Denise-Spring	L. Rigg	LD 2000	30.00	45.00
1995-01-009	Melissa-Autumn	L. Rigg	LD 2000	30.00	45.00
1995-01-010	Emily-Summer	L. Rigg	LD 2000	30.00	45.00
1995-01-011	Carol-Winter	L. Rigg	LD 2000	30.00	45.00
1995-01-012	Amy	L. Rigg	LD 5000	15.00	30.00
1995-01-013	Rachel	L. Rigg	LD 5000	15.00	30.00
1995-01-014	Angela	L. Rigg	LD 5000	15.00	30.00
1995-01-015	Carrie	L. Rigg	LD 5000	15.00	30.00
1995-01-016	Debra	L. Rigg	LD 5000	15.00	30.00
1995-01-017	Muriel	L. Rigg	LD 5000	15.00	30.00
1995-01-018	Thomas	L. Rigg	LD 2000	30.00	45.00
1995-01-019	Beth	L. Rigg	LD 2000	30.00	45.00
1995-01-020	Mrs. Claus	L. Rigg	LD 2000	30.00	45.00
1995-01-021	Santa Claus	L. Rigg	LD 2000	30.00	45.00
1995-01-022	Mary Louise	L. Rigg	LD 2000	30.00	45.00
1995-01-023	Frances	L. Rigg	LD 2000	30.00	45.00
1995-01-024	Shawine	L. Rigg	LD 2000	30.00	45.00
1995-01-025	Nathan	L. Rigg	LD 2000	30.00	45.00

ENESCO® CORPORATION – CENTIMENTAL BEARS

RELEASE YEAR	FIGURINE	ARTIST	EDITION	ISSUE	QUOTE
1995-01-001	Jilly 116548	P. Fagen	OP	10.00	10.00
1995-01-002	Morris Minor 116785	P. Fagen	OP	10.00	10.00
1995-01-003	Chocolate Chip 116807	P. Fagen	OP	5.00	5.00
1995-01-004	Joseph 116823	P. Fagen	OP	5.00	5.00
1995-01-005	Teddy Robinson 116831	P. Fagen	OP	5.00	5.00
1995-01-006	Bernard 116947	P. Fagen	OP	10.00	10.00
1995-01-007	Clarissa 117374	P. Fagen	OP	12.50	12.50
1995-01-008	Burt 122378	P. Fagen	OP	5.00	5.00
1995-01-009	William 122386	P. Fagen	OP	12.50	12.50
1995-01-010	Jack 122416	P. Fagen	OP	17.50	17.50
1995-01-011	Miranda 122424	P. Fagen	OP	17.50	17.50
1995-01-012	The Happy Couple 122440	P. Fagen	OP	17.50	17.50
1995-01-013	Violet 125717	P. Fagen	OP	5.00	5.00
1995-01-014	Adrian 125725	P. Fagen	OP	12.50	12.50

Enesco® Corporation – CENTIMENTAL BEARS

Release Year	Figurine	Artist	Edition	Issue	Quote
1995-01-015	Peter Bear 116289	P. Fagen	OP	10.00	10.00
1995-01-016	Arabella 116300	P. Fagen	OP	12.50	12.50
1995-01-017	Christopher & Gustav 116319	P. Fagen	OP	12.50	12.50
1995-01-018	Timmy 116327	P. Fagen	OP	12.50	12.50
1995-01-019	Regina 116343	P. Fagen	OP	10.00	10.00
1995-01-020	Kenny 116351	P. Fagen	OP	12.50	12.50
1995-01-021	Ian 116513	P. Fagen	OP	10.00	10.00
1995-01-022	Elly May 116521	P. Fagen	OP	12.50	12.50
1995-01-023	Nym's Black Cat 145122	P. Fagen	OP	10.00	10.00
1995-01-024	Binkie's Pumpkin 145130	P. Fagen	OP	12.50	12.50
1995-01-025	Meekie's Lantern 145149	P. Fagen	OP	12.50	12.50
1995-01-026	Spooky Ralph 145157	P. Fagen	OP	10.00	10.00
1995-01-027	Sopwith Gets Ready 145165	P. Fagen	OP	10.00	10.00
1995-01-028	Wizzard Litmus 145173	P. Fagen	OP	10.00	10.00
1995-01-029	Reggie "The Halloween Bandit" 145181	P. Fagen	OP	10.00	10.00
1995-01-030	Irvine's Trick or Treat 145203	P. Fagen	OP	10.00	10.00
1995-01-031	Squidge 145254	P. Fagen	OP	5.00	5.00
1995-01-032	Baron Von Berne 145262	P. Fagen	OP	17.50	17.50
1995-01-033	Sullivan 145270	P. Fagen	OP	12.50	12.50
1995-01-034	Ollie 145289	P. Fagen	OP	17.50	17.50
1995-01-035	Mr. Perkins 145297	P. Fagen	OP	10.00	10.00
1995-01-036	Vernon 145300	P. Fagen	OP	10.00	10.00
1995-01-037	Red Bear 145319	P. Fagen	OP	10.00	10.00
1995-01-038	Emlyn 145327	P. Fagen	OP	17.50	17.50
1995-01-039	Cousin Eccy 145335	P. Fagen	OP	5.00	5.00
1995-01-040	Bruno 145343	P. Fagen	OP	12.50	12.50

Enesco® Corporation – PENNY WHISTLE LANE

Release Year	Figurine	Artist	Edition	Issue	Quote
1994-01-201	Trinkets Drum 655384	P. Fagen	OP	15.00	15.00
1994-01-202	James 655392	P. Fagen	OP	10.00	10.00
1994-01-203	Popsey 655376	P. Fagen	OP	10.00	10.00
1994-01-204	Ben 657948	P. Fagen	OP	5.00	5.00
1994-01-205	Davey 657956	P. Fagen	OP	5.00	5.00
1994-01-206	George 657980	P. Fagen	OP	10.00	10.00
1994-01-207	Binky 657921	P. Fagen	OP	5.00	5.00
1994-01-208	Prudence 657832	P. Fagen	OP	10.00	10.00
1995-01-209	Letter To Santa 145114	P. Fagen	OP	65.00	65.00
1995-01-210	Trunk Of Teddies 128678	P. Fagen	LD 1000	60.00	65-75.00
1995-01-211	Jingles Better Bear 127892	P. Fagen	OP	10.00	10.00
1995-01-212	Priscilla 114367	P. Fagen	OP	10.00	10.00

Fort®, Inc. – JOY BEARS™

Release Year	Figurine	Artist	Edition	Issue	Quote
1994-01-001	Sis	S. Slother	OP	15.00	15.00
1994-01-002	Topper	S. Slother	OP	15.00	15.00
1994-01-003	Cubby	S. Slother	OP	15.00	15.00
1994-01-006	Reach For The Stars	S. Slother	OP	20.00	20.00
1994-01-007	Mr. Snowbear	S. Slother	OP	20.00	20.00
1994-01-008	Rollie	S. Slother	OP	15.00	15.00
1994-01-009	Bundled Up	S. Slother	OP	15.00	15.00
1994-01-011	Do-Re-Mi	S. Slother	OP	15.00	15.00
1994-01-013	Joyful Surprise	S. Slother	OP	15.00	15.00
1994-01-015	Joyous Snooze	S. Slother	OP	40.00	40.00
1994-01-017	Flyin'	S. Slother	OP	15.00	15.00
1994-01-018	Ooops	S. Slother	OP	15.00	15.00
1994-01-019	Open Arms	S. Slother	OP	15.00	15.00
1994-01-021	Cooky	S. Slother	OP	15.00	15.00
1994-01-022	Just Checkin'	S. Slother	OP	15.00	15.00
1994-01-023	Rockin	S. Slother	OP	20.00	20.00
1994-01-024	Just Wishin'	S. Slother	OP	15.00	15.00
1994-01-025	Giddy-Up	S. Slother	OP	20.00	20.00
1994-01-026	Shades	S. Slother	OP	15.00	15.00
1994-01-028	Little Bit	S. Slother	OP	15.00	15.00
1994-01-029	Struttin'	S. Slother	OP	15.00	15.00
1994-01-030	Nighty Night	S. Slother	OP	40.00	40.00

FORT®, INC. – JOY BEARS™

RELEASE YEAR	FIGURINE	ARTIST	EDITION	ISSUE	QUOTE
Accessories:					
1994-01-004	Lamp Post	S. Slother	OP	15.00	15.00
1994-01-005	Tree	S. Slother	OP	20.00	20.00
1994-01-010	Piano	S. Slother	OP	40.00	40.00
1994-01-012	Couch	S. Slother	OP	40.00	40.00
1994-01-014	Fireplace	S. Slother	OP	50.00	50.00
1994-01-016	Skating Pond	S. Slother	OP	45.00	45.00
1994-01-020	Gazebo	S. Slother	OP	50.00	50.00
1994-01-027	Rug	S. Slother	OP	20.00	20.00

THE FRANKLIN MINT

RELEASE YEAR	FIGURINE	ARTIST	EDITION	ISSUE	QUOTE
	The Teddy Bear Tribute Collection	The Franklin Mint	UD for Print		
	Teddy Town Player Sculpture Collection	Carol Lawson	UD for Print		No
	Hotel Teddington Collection	Carol Lawson	UD for Print		prices
	The Teddy Bear Picnic	Carol Lawson	UD for Print		available
	Teddy Bear Wedding	Carol Lawson	UD for Print		
	A Stitch In Time	Carol Lawson	UD for Print		

GANZ, INC. – GRANDMA'S ATTIC™

RELEASE YEAR	FIGURINE	ARTIST	EDITION	ISSUE	QUOTE
1994-01-101	Coco & Jiffy	C. Thammavongsa	OP	11.00	11.00
1994-01-102	Dilly-Dally	C.Thammavongsa	OP	13.50	13.50
1994-01-104	Too Too	C. Thammavongsa	OP	10.00	10.00
1995-01-105	Molly-Coddle	C. Thammavongsa	OP	16.00	16.00
1995-01-106	Crumples & Cream Puff	C. Thammavongsa	OP	13.50	13.50
1995-01-108	Bumblebeary	C. Thammavongsa	OP	10.00	10.00
1995-01-109	Balderdash	D. Thammavongsa	OP	25.00	25.00
1995-01-110	Jelly-Belly	C. Thammavongsa	OP	12.00	12.00
1995-01-111	Sprinkles	C. Thammavongsa	OP	15.00	15.00
1995-01-112	Prince Fuddle-Duddle & Princess Dazzle	C. Thammavongsa	OP	17.00	17.00
1995-01-113	Dumblekin	C. Thammavongsa	OP	19.00	19.00
1995-01-201	Cuddles	C. Thammavongsa	OP	12.00	12.00
1995-01-202	Abracadabra	C. Thammavongsa	OP	14.00	14.00
1995-01-203	Tickles and Giggles	C. Thammavongsa	OP	20.00	20.00
1995-01-204	Skippy & Marmalade	C. Thammavongsa	OP	23.00	23.00
1995-01-301	Hucklebeary	C. Thammavongsa	OP	14.50	14.50
1995-01-302	Slugger	C. Thammavongsa	OP	13.00	13.00
1995-01-303	Lamble Pie	C. Thammavongsa	OP	14.50	14.50

GANZ, INC. – COTTAGE COLLECTIBLES®

RELEASE YEAR	FIGURINE	ARTIST	EDITION	ISSUE	QUOTE
1995-01-2001	School Days	C. Lagerwegij/J. Mallett/L. Moritz	OP	16.00	16.00
1995-01-2002	Goin' Fishin'	C. Lagerwegij/J. Mallett/L. Moritz	OP	16.00	16.00
1995-01-2003	My Favorite Things	C. Lagerwegij/J. Mallett/L. Moritz	OP	16.00	16.00
1995-01-2004	Grandma's Treasures	C. Lagerwegij/J. Mallett/L. Moritz	OP	25.00	25.00
1995-01-2005	Naptime	C. Lagerwegij/J. Mallett/L. Moritz	OP	23.00	23.00
1995-01-2006	Tea Time	C. Lagerwegij/J. Mallett/L. Moritz	OP	23.00	23.00
1995-01-2007	Best Friends	C. Lagerwegij/J. Mallett/L. Moritz	OP	16.00	16.00
1995-01-2008	Circus Parade	C. Lagerwegij/J. Mallett/L. Moritz	OP	23.00	23.00
1995-01-2009	First Love	C. Lagerwegij/J. Mallett/L. Moritz	OP	20.00	20.00
1995-01-2010	Bath Time	C. Lagerwegij/J. Mallett/L. Moritz	OP	17.00	17.00
1995-01-2011	Play Time	C. Lagerwegij/J. Mallett/L. Moritz	OP	23.00	23.00
1995-01-2013	A Job Well Done	C. Lagerwegij/J. Mallett/L. Moritz	OP	25.00	25.00

GREAT AMERICAN® TAYLOR COLLECTIBLES CORPORATION – TAYLOR BEAR FAMILY

RELEASE YEAR	FIGURINE	ARTIST	EDITION	ISSUE	QUOTE
1982-01-100	Marcie 80S	G. Snow	RT 1989	19.00	35.00
1982-01-101	Glyn 81SB	G. Snow	RT 1989	19.00	35.00
1982-01-102	Beauregard 82SR	G. Snow	RT 1989	16.00	28.00
1982-01-103	Elizabeth 83SB	G. Snow	RT 1989	16.00	28.00
1982-01-104	Sidney 84SR	G. Snow	RT 1989	10.00	25.00
1982-01-105	Suzy 85SB	G. Snow	RT 1989	10.00	25.00

GREAT AMERICAN® TAYLOR COLLECTIBLES CORPORATION – TAYLOR BEAR FAMILY - SERIES TB2

RELEASE YEAR	FIGURINE	ARTIST	EDITION	ISSUE	QUOTE
1996-02-106	Marcie TB2	G. Snow	OP	UD for Print	
1996-02-107	Glyn TB2	G. Snow	OP	UD for Print	
1996-02-108	Beauregard TB2	G. Snow	OP	UD for Print	

Great American® Taylor Collectibles Corporation – TAYLOR BEAR FAMILY - SERIES TB2

Release Year	Figurine	Artist	Edition	Issue	Quote
1996-02-109	Elizabeth TB2	G. Snow	OP	UD for Print	
1996-02-110	Sidney TB2	G. Snow	OP	UD for Print	
1996-02-110	Suzy TB2	G. Snow	OP	UD for Print	

L. L. Knickerbocker Company – 75TH ANNIVERSARY HISTORICAL HOUSE OF BEARS

Release Year	Figurine	Artist	Edition	Issue	Quote
1995-01-11401-1	Papa Bear	K. Cropper	RT 1997	25.00	25.00
1995-01-11401-2	Mama Bear	K. Cropper	RT 1997	25.00	25.00
1995-01-11401-3	Smokey Bear	L. Grucza	RT 1997	25.00	25.00

L. L. Knickerbocker Company – 75TH ANNIVERSARY HISTORICAL HOUSE OF BEARS

Release Year	Figurine	Artist	Edition	Issue	Quote
1995-01-11401-4	Brother Bear	K. Cropper	RT 1997	25.00	25.00
1995-01-11401-5	Mimmi Bear	K. Cropper	RT 1997	25.00	25.00
1995-01-11401-6	Sister Bear	K. Cropper	RT 1997	25.00	25.00
1995-01-11400-0	Anniversary House Display	K. Cropper	RT 1997 Available Through Collection Only		

Nevenschwander Artworks – BREAD N' BUTTER BEARS

Release Year	Figurine	Artist	Edition	Issue	Quote
1988-01-001	School Boy	R. & L. Nevenschwander	OP	48.50	48.50
1988-01-002	Papa	R. & L. Nevenschwander	OP	48.50	48.50
1988-01-003	Mama	R. & L. Nevenschwander	OP	48.50	48.50
1988-01-004	Cowboy	R. & L. Nevenschwander	OP	48.50	48.50
1988-01-005	Hobo	R. & L. Nevenschwander	OP	48.50	48.50
1988-01-006	Santa Bear	R. & L. Nevenschwander	OP	57.50	57.50
1988-01-007	Mrs. Claus Bear	R. & L. Nevenschwander	OP	57.50	57.50
1994-01-008	Teddy Roosevelt & Roughrider	R. & L. Nevenschwander	OP	57.50	57.50
1994-01-009	Teddy Roosevelt Presidential	R. & L. Nevenschwander	OP	57.50	57.50
1994-01-010	Logo Bear Collector Club	R. & L. Nevenschwander			
1995-01-011	Mini Date Bear	R. & L. Nevenschwander	OP	37.50	37.50
1995-01-012	Mini Cowboy	R. & L. Nevenschwander	OP	38.50	38.50
1995-01-013	Abearham Lincoln	R. & L. Nevenschwander	OP	61.50	61.50

North American Bear Co., Inc. – MUFFY VANDERBEAR COLLECTION

Release Year	Figurine	Artist	Edition	Issue	Quote
1989-01-700	Bearb Ruth	In-House	RT 1992	11.00	25.00
1989-01-701	Bearilyn Monroe	In-House	RT 1992	11.00	25.00
1989-01-703	Clara Bearton	In-House	RT 1992	11.00	25.00
1989-01-704	Dr. KilBear	In-House	RT 1992	11.00	25.00
1989-01-705	Humphrey Beargart I	In-House	RT 1992	11.00	25.00
1989-01-706	Lauren Bearcall	In-House	RT 1992	11.00	25.00
1989-01-707	Rhett Beartler	In-House	RT 1992	11.00	25.00
1989-01-708	Scarlett O'Beara II	In-House	RT 1992	11.00	25.00
1990-01-711	Anna Bearvolua	In-House	RT 1992	11.00	25.00
1990-01-712	Amelia Bearhart	In-House	RT 1992	11.00	25.00
1990-01-713	William Shakesbear	In-House	RT 1992	11.00	25.00
1992-01-719	Alice In Wonbearland	In-House	RT 1992	12.00	30.00
1992-01-720	Cinbearella	In-House	RT 1992	12.00	30.00
1992-01-721	Snow Bear	In-House	RT 1992	12.00	30.00
1994-01-5013	Muffy Day In The Country	In-House	OP	12.00	12.00
1994-01-5014	Muffy Gibearny	In-House	OP	12.00	12.00
1994-01-5015	Muffy High Tea	In-House	OP	12.00	12.00
1994-01-5016	Muffy Safari	In-House	OP	12.00	12.00
1994-01-5017	Muffy Sailor	In-House	OP	12.00	12.00

Pacific Rim Import Corporation – PUDDLEBROOK® TEDDIES

Release Year	Figurine	Artist	Edition	Issue	Quote
1995-01-50023-01	Taking A Tumble	P. Sebern	OP	10.00	10.00
1995-01-50023-02	Sleiding Fun	P. Sebern	OP	10.00	10.00
1995-01-50023-03	Ice Dancers	P. Sebern	OP	10.00	10.00
1995-01-50023-04	Collecting The Tree	P. Sebern	OP	10.00	10.00

Penni Jo Originals – PENNIBEARS™

Release Year	Figurine	Artist	Edition	Issue	Quote
1989-08-001	Bouquet Girl PB-001	P. J. Jonas	RT	20.00	45-50.00
1989-08-002	Honey Bear PB-002	P. J. Jonas	RT	20.00	45-50.00
1989-08-003	Bouquet Boy PB-003	P. J. Jonas	RT	20.00	45-50.00
1989-08-004	Beautiful Bride PB-004	P. J. Jonas	RT	20.00	45-50.00
1989-08-005	Butterfly Bear PB-005	P. J. Jonas	RT	20.00	45-50.00

RELEASE YEAR	FIGURINE	ARTIST	EDITION	ISSUE	QUOTE
1989-08-006	Cookie Bandit PB-006	P. J. Jonas	RT	20.00	22.00
1989-08-007	Baby Hugs PB-007	P. J. Jonas	RT	20.00	35.00
1989-08-008	Doctor Bear PB-008	P. J. Jonas	RT	20.00	22.00
1989-08-009	Lazy Days PB-009	P. J. Jonas	RT	20.00	22.00
1989-08-010	Petite Mademoiselle PB-010	P. J. Jonas	RT	20.00	45.00
1990-08-011	Giddyup Teddy PB-011	P. J. Jonas	RT	20.00	35-50.00
1990-08-012	Buttons & Bows PB-012	P. J. Jonas	RT	20.00	45-50.00
1990-08-013	Country Spring PB-013	P. J. Jonas	RT	20.00	45-50.00
1990-08-014	Garden Path PB-104	P. J. Jonas	RT	20.00	45-50.00
1989-08-015	Handsome Groom PB-015	P. J. Jonas	RT	20.00	45.00
1989-08-016	Nap Time PB-016	P. J. Jonas	RT	20.00	22.00
1989-08-017	Nurse Bear PB-017	P. J. Jonas	RT	20.00	22.00
1989-08-018	Birthday Bear PB-018	P. J. Jonas	RT	20.00	40.00
1989-08-019	Attic Fun PB-019	P. J. Jonas	RT	20.00	30.00
1989-08-020	Puppy Bath PB-020	P. J. Jonas	RT	20.00	22.00
1989-08-021	Puppy Love PB-021	P. J. Jonas	RT	20.00	22.00
1989-08-022	Tubby Teddy PB-022	P. J. Jonas	RT	20.00	22.00
1989-08-023	Bathtime Buddies PB-023	P. J. Jonas	RT	20.00	22.00
1989-08-024	Southern Belle PB-024	P. J. Jonas	RT	20.00	45-50.00
1990-08-025	Boooo Bear PB-025	P. J. Jonas	RT	20.00	22.00
1990-08-026	Sneaky Snowball PB-026	P. J. Jonas	RT	20.00	22.00
1990-08-027	Count Bearacula PB-027	P. J. Jonas	RT	22.00	24.00
1990-08-028	Dress Up Fun PB-028	P. J. Jonas	RT	22.00	24.00
1990-08-029	Scarecrow Teddy PB-029	P. J. Jonas	RT	24.00	24.00
1990-08-030	Country Quilter PB-030	P. J. Jonas	RT	22.00	26.00
1990-08-031	Santa Bear-ing Gifts PB-031	P. J. Jonas	RT	24.00	26.00
1990-08-032	Stocking Surprise PB-032	P. J. Jonas	RT	22.00	26.00
1991-08-033	Bearly Awake PB-033	P. J. Jonas	RT	22.00	22.00
1991-08-034	Lil' Merteddy PB-034	P. J. Jonas	RT	24.00	24.00
1991-08-035	Bump-bear-Crop PB-035	P. J. Jonas	RT	26.00	26.00
1991-08-036	Country Lullabye PB-036	P. J. Jonas	RT	24.00	24.00
1991-08-037	Bear Footin' it PB-037	P. J. Jonas	RT	24.00	24.00
1991-08-038	Windy Day PB-038	P. J. Jonas	RT	24.00	24.00
1991-08-039	Summer Sailing PB-039	P. J. Jonas	RT	26.00	26.00
1991-08-040	Goodnight Sweet Princess PB-040	P. J. Jonas	RT	26.00	26.00
1991-08-041	Goodnight Little Prince PB-041	P. J. Jonas	RT	26.00	26.00
1991-08-042	Bunny Buddies PB-042	P. J. Jonas	RT	22.00	22.00
1991-08-043	Baking Goodies PB-043	P. J. Jonas	RT	26.00	26.00
1991-08-044	Sweetheart Bears PB-044	P. J. Jonas	RT	28.00	28.00
1991-08-045	Bountiful Harvest PB-045	P. J. Jonas	RT	24.00	24.00
1991-08-046	Christmas Reinbear PB-046	P. J. Jonas	RT	28.00	28.00
1991-08-047	Pilgrim Provider PBB-047	P. J. Jonas	RT	32.00	32.00
1991-08-048	Sweet Lil' Sis PB-048	P. J. Jonas	RT	22.00	20.00
1991-08-049	Curtain Call PB-049	P. J. Jonas	RT	24.00	24.00
1991-08-050	Boo Hoo Bear PB-050	P. J. Jonas	RT	22.00	22.00
1991-08-051	Happy Hobo PB-051	P. J. Jonas	RT	26.00	26.00
1991-08-052	A Wild Ride PB-052	P. J. Jonas	RT	26.00	26.00
1992-08-053	Spanish Rose PB-053	P. J. Jonas	12/94	24.00	24.00
1992-08-054	Tally Ho! PB-054	P. J. Jonas	12/94	22.00	22.00
1992-08-055	Smokey's Nephew PB-055	P. J. Jonas	12/94	22.00	22.00
1992-08-056	Cinderella PB-056	P. J. Jonas	12/94	22.00	22.00
1992-08-057	Puddle Jumper PB-057	P. J. Jonas	12/94	24.00	24.00
1992-08-058	After Every Meal PB-058	P. J. Jonas	12/94	22.00	22.00
1992-08-059	Pot O' Gold PB-059	P. J. Jonas	12/94	22.00	22.00
1992-08-060	I Made It Girl PB-060	P. J. Jonas	12/94	22.00	22.00
1992-08-061	I Made It Boy PB-061	P. J. Jonas	12/94	22.00	22.00
1992-08-062	Dust Bunny Roundup PB-062	P. J. Jonas	12/94	22.00	22.00
1992-08-063	Sandbox Fun PB-063	P. J. Jonas	12/94	22.00	22.00
1992-08-064	First Prom PB-064	P. J. Jonas	12/94	22.00	22.00
1992-08-065	Clowning Around PB-065	P. J. Jonas	12/94	22.00	22.00
1992-08-066	Batter Up PB-066	P. J. Jonas	12/94	22.00	22.00
1992-08-067	Will You Be Mine? PB-067	P. J. Jonas	12/94	22.00	22.00
1992-08-068	On Your Toes PB-068	P. J. Jonas	12/94	24.00	24.00
1992-08-069	Apple For Teacher PB-069	P. J. Jonas	12/94	24.00	24.00
1992-08-070	Downhill Thrills PB-070	P. J. Jonas	12/94	24.00	24.00
1992-08-071	Lil' Devil PB-071	P. J. Jonas	12/94	24.00	24.00
1992-08-072	Touchdown PB-072	P. J. Jonas	12/94	22.00	22.00
1992-08-073	Bear-Capade PB-073	P. J. Jonas	12/94	22.00	22.00
1992-08-074	Lil' Sis Makes Up PB-074	P. J. Jonas	12/94	22.00	22.00
1992-08-075	Christmas Cookies PB-075	P. J. Jonas	12/94	22.00	22.00
1992-08-076	Decorating The Wreath PB-076	P. J. Jonas	12/94	22.00	22.00

Penni Jo Originals – PENNIBEARS™

Release Year	Figurine	Artist	Edition	Issue	Quote
1993-08-077	A Happy Camper PB-077	P. J. Jonas	12/95	28.00	28.00
1993-08-078	My Forever Love PB-078	P. J. Jonas	12/95	28.00	28.00
1993-08-079	Rest Stop PB-079	P. J. Jonas	12/95	24.00	24.00
1993-08-080	May Joy Be Yours PB-080	P. J. Jonas	12/95	24.00	24.00
1993-08-081	Santa's Helpers PB-081	P. J. Jonas	12/95	28.00	28.00
1993-08-082	Gotta Try Again PB-082	P. J. Jonas	12/95	24.00	24.00
1993-08-083	Little Bear Peep PB-083	P. J. Jonas	12/95	24.00	24.00
1993-08-084	Happy Birthday PB-084	P. J. Jonas	12/95	26.00	26.00
1993-08-085	Getting 'Round On My Own PB-085	P. J. Jonas	12/95	26.00	26.00
1993-08-086	Summer Belle PB-086	P. J. Jonas	12/95	24.00	24.00
1993-08-087	Making It Better PB-087	P. J. Jonas	12/95	24.00	24.00
1993-08-088	Big Chief Little Bear PB-088	P. J. Jonas	12/95	28.00	28.00
1994-08-089	Winter Friends PB-089	P. J. Jonas	OP	26.00	26.00
1994-08-090	Aunt Victoria PB-090	P. J. Jonas	OP	22.50	22.50
1994-08-091	Lily Pad Surprise PB-091	P. J. Jonas	OP	24.00	24.00
1994-08-092	Two By Two PB-092	P. J. Jonas	OP	23.00	23.00
1994-08-093	Saint -AHH PB-093	P. J. Jonas	OP	30.00	30.00
1994-08-094	Victorian Foundations PB-094	P. J. Jonas	OP	22.00	22.00
1994-08-095	The Frog Princess PB-095	P. J. Jonas	OP	26.00	26.00

Penni Jo Originals – PENNIBEARS™ COLLECTOR'S CLUB MEMBERS ONLY EDITIONS

Release Year	Figurine	Artist	Edition	Issue	Quote
1991-09-001	First Collection PB-C90	P. J. Jonas	RT	26.00	100-125.00
1992-09-002	Collecting Makes Cents PB-C91	P. J. Jonas	RT	26.00	75-150.00
1992-09-003	Today's Pleasures, Tommorrow's Treasures	P. J. Jonas	RT	26.00	100.00
1993-09-004	Chalkin Up Another Year PBC-93	P. J. Jonas	RT	26.00	26.00
1994-09-005	Artist's Touch-Collector's Treasurer PBC-94	P. J. Jonas	Yr.Iss.	26.00	26.00

Raikes Originals – RAVENWOOD COLLECTION

Release Year	Figurine	Artist	Edition	Issue	Quote
1995-01-0001	Gweena	R. Raikes	LD/OP	UD	UD
1995-01-0002	Martin	R. Raikes	LD/OP	UD	UD
1995-01-0003	Willie	R. Raikes	LD/OP	UD	UD
1995-01-0004	Morris	R. Raikes	LD/OP	UD	UD
1995-01-0005	Larkin	R. Raikes	LD/OP	UD	UD
1995-01-0006	Warren	R. Raikes	LD/OP	UD	UD

Russ® Berrie and Company – TEDDYTOWN™ SCULPTSTONE FIGURINE COLLECTION

Release Year	Figurine	Artist	Edition	Issue	Quote
1994-01-13715	Jester	In-House	RT12/94	9.00	14.00
1994-01-13716	Le Artiste	In-House	RT12/94	9.00	14.00
1994-01-13730	Springtime Girl	In-House	RT12/94	8.00	12.00
1994-01-13731	Get Well Soon	In-House	RT12/94	8.00	12.00
1994-01-13732	Small Ballerina	In-House	RT12/94	8.00	12.00
1994-01-13733	Nighty, Night Girl	In-House	RT12/94	8.00	12.00
1994-01-13734	Executive	In-House	RT12/94	8.00	12.00
1994-01-13735	Small Groom	In-House	RT12/94	8.00	12.00
1994-01-13736	Small Bride	In-House	RT12/94	10.00	15.00
1994-01-13737	Happy Birthday Clown	In-House	RT12/94	8.00	12.00
1994-01-13738	Nurse	In-House	RT12/94	8.00	12.00
1994-01-13740	Winter Girl	In-House	RT12/94	10.00	15.00
1994-01-13741	Pilot	In-House	RT12/94	9.00	14.00
1994-01-13742	Golfer	In-House	RT12/94	9.00	14.00
1994-01-13743	"I Love You" Boy	In-House	RT12/94	9.00	14.00
1994-01-13744	"I Love You" Girl	In-House	RT12/94	9.00	14.00
1994-01-13745	Raincoat	In-House	RT12/94	9.00	14.00
1994-01-13746	Sunshine	In-House	RT12/94	9.00	14.00
1994-01-13747	P. J. Boy	In-House	RT12/94	9.00	14.00
1994-01-13748	P. J. Girl	In-House	RT12/94	9.00	14.00
1994-01-13749	1st Communion Boy	In-House	RT12/94	9.00	14.00
1994-01-13750	1st Communion Girl	In-House	RT12/94	10.00	15.00
1994-01-13751	Sailor Girl	In-House	RT12/94	9.00	14.00
1994-01-13752	School Girl	In-House	RT12/94	9.00	14.00
1994-01-13753	School Boy	In-House	RT12/94	9.00	14.00
1994-01-13754	Country Girl Plaid	In-House	RT12/94	10.00	15.00
1994-01-13755	Fisherman	In-House	RT12/94	10.00	15.00
1994-01-13756	Winterboy	In-House	RT12/94	9.00	14.00
1994-01-13757	School Girl	In-House	RT12/94	9.00	14.00
1994-01-13758	Country Girl	In-House	RT12/94	9.00	14.00
1994-01-13759	Country Boy	In-House	RT12/94	10.00	15.00
1994-01-13760	Sheriff	In-House	RT12/94		

RELEASE YEAR	FIGURINE	ARTIST	EDITION	ISSUE	QUOTE
1994-01-13761	Prep School Girl	In-House	RT12/94	10.00	15.00
1994-01-13780	Santa Bear	In-House	RT12/94	9.00	14.00
1994-01-13765-1	Napoleon	In-House	RT12/94	8.00	12.00
1994-01-13765-2	Musketeer	In-House	RT12/94	8.00	12.00
1994-01-13765-3	Princess	In-House	RT12/94	8.00	12.00
1994-01-13765-4	Lady-In-Waiting	In-House	RT12/94	8.00	12.00
1994-01-13761	Prep School Girl	In-House	RT12/94	10.00	15.00
1994-01-13739	Sherlock	In-House	RT12/94	10.00	15.00
1994-01-13762	Royal Guard	In-House	RT12/94	10.00	15.00
1994-01-13763	Robin	In-House	RT12/94	10.00	15.00
1994-01-13764	Genie	In-House	RT12/94	9.00	14.00
1994-01-13767	Peter	In-House	RT12/94	9.00	14.00
1994-01-13768	Little Bo Peep	In-House	RT12/94	10.00	15.00
1994-01-14289	Victorian Boy	In-House	RT12/94	9.00	14.00
1994-01-14290	Victorian Girl	In-House	RT12/94	9.00	14.00
1995-02-13730	Springtime Girl	In-House	RT12/95	8.00	12.00
1995-02-13731	Get Well Soon	In-House	RT12/95	8.00	12.00
1995-02-13732	Small Ballerina	In-House	RT12/95	8.00	12.00
1995-02-13733	Nighty, Night Girl	In-House	RT12/95	8.00	12.00
1995-02-13734	Executive	In-House	RT12/95	8.00	12.00
1995-02-13735	Small Groom	In-House	RT12/95	8.00	12.00
1995-02-13736	Small Bride	In-House	RT12/95	10.00	15.00
1995-02-13737	Happy Birthday Clown	In-House	RT12/95	8.00	12.00
1995-02-13738	Nurse	In-House	RT12/95	8.00	12.00
1995-02-13740	Winter Girl	In-House	RT12/95	10.00	15.00
1995-02-14289	Victorian Boy	In-House	RT12/95	9.00	14.00
1995-02-14290	Victorian Girl	In-House	RT12/95	9.00	14.00
1995-02-13741	Pilot	In-House	RT12/95	9.00	14.00
1995-02-13742	Golfer	In-House	RT12/95	9.00	14.00
1995-02-13743	"I Love You" Boy	In-House	RT12/95	9.00	14.00
1995-02-13744	"I Love You" Girl	In-House	RT12/95	9.00	14.00
1995-02-13745	Rainwear	In-House	RT12/95	9.00	14.00
1995-02-13746	Sunshine	In-House	RT12/95	9.00	14.00
1995-02-13747	P. J. Boy	In-House	RT12/95	9.00	14.00
1995-02-13748	P. J. Girl	In-House	RT12/95	9.00	14.00
1995-02-13749	1st Communion Boy	In-House	RT12/95	9.00	14.00
1995-02-13750	1st Communion Girl	In-House	RT12/95	9.00	14.00
1995-02-13751	Sailor Girl	In-House	RT12/95	10.00	15.00
1995-02-13752	School Girl	In-House	RT12/95	9.00	14.00
1995-02-13753	School Boy	In-House	RT12/95	9.00	14.00
1995-02-13754	Country Girl Plaid	In-House	RT12/95	9.00	14.00
1995-02-13755	Fisherman	In-House	RT12/95	10.00	15.00
1995-02-13756	Winter Boy	In-House	RT12/95	10.00	15.00
1995-02-13757	School Girl	In-House	RT12/95	9.00	14.00
1995-02-13758	Country Girl	In-House	RT12/95	9.00	14.00
1995-02-13759	Country Boy	In-House	RT12/95	9.00	14.00
1995-02-13760	Sheriff	In-House	RT12/95	10.00	15.00
1995-02-13761	Prep School Girl	In-House	RT12/95	10.00	15.00
1995-02-13780	Santa Bear	In-House	RT12/95	9.00	14.00
1995-02-13765-1	Napoleon	In-House	RT12/95	8.00	12.00
1995-02-13765-2	Musketeer	In-House	RT12/95	8.00	12.00
1995-02-13765-3	Princess	In-House	RT12/95	8.00	12.00
1995-02-13765-4	Lady-In-Waiting	In-House	RT12/95	8.00	12.00
1995-02-13761	Prep School Girl	In-House	RT12/95	10.00	15.00
1995-02-13739	Sherlock	In-House	RT12/95	10.00	15.00
1995-02-13762	Royal Guard	In-House	RT12/95	10.00	15.00
1995-02-13763	Robin	In-House	RT12/95	10.00	15.00
1995-02-13764	Genie	In-House	RT12/95	9.00	14.00
1995-02-13767	Peter	In-House	RT12/95	9.00	14.00
1995-02-13768	Little Bo Peep	In-House	RT12/95	10.00	15.00
1995-02-13715	Jester	In-House	RT12/95	9.00	14.00
1995-02-13716	Le Artiste	In-House	RT12/95	9.00	14.00
1995-01-13831	Ballerina	In-House	OP	6.00	6.00
1995-01-13832	Birthday Boy	In-House	OP	6.00	6.00
1995-01-13833	Birthday Girl	In-House	OP	6.00	6.00
1995-01-13838	Wedding Bears	In-House	OP	6.00	6.00
1995-01-13839	25th Anniversary	In-House	OP	6.00	6.00

RUSS® BERRIE AND COMPANY – TEDDYTOWN™ SCULPTSTONE FIGURINE COLLECTION

RELEASE YEAR	FIGURINE	ARTIST	EDITION	ISSUE	QUOTE
1995-01-13841	50th Anniversary	In-House	OP	6.00	6.00
1996-03-13730	Springtime Girl	In-House	OP	9.00	12.00
1996-03-13731	Get Well Soon	In-House	OP	9.00	12.00
1996-03-13732	Small Ballerina	In-House	OP	9.00	12.00
1996-03-13733	Nighty, Night Girl	In-House	OP	9.00	12.00
1996-03-13734	Executive	In-House	OP	9.00	12.00
1996-03-13735	Small Groom	In-House	OP	9.00	12.00
1996-03-13736	Small Bride	In-House	OP	10.00	15.00
1996-03-13737	Happy Birthday Clown	In-House	OP	9.00	12.00
1996-03-13738	Nurse	In-House	OP	9.00	12.00
1996-03-13740	Winter Girl	In-House	OP	10.00	15.00
1996-03-14289	Victorian Boy	In-House	OP	9.00	14.00
1996-03-14290	Victorian Girl	In-House	OP	9.00	14.00
1996-03-13741	Pilot	In-House	OP	9.00	14.00
1996-03-13742	Golfer	In-House	OP	9.00	14.00
1996-03-13743	"I Love You" Boy	In-House	OP	9.00	14.00
1996-03-13744	"I Love You" Girl	In-House	OP	9.00	14.00
1996-03-13745	Rainwear	In-House	OP	9.00	14.00
1996-03-13746	Sunshine	In-House	OP	9.00	14.00
1996-03-13747	P. J. Boy	In-House	OP	9.00	14.00
1996-03-13748	P. J. Girl	In-House	OP	9.00	14.00
1996-03-13749	1st Communion Boy	In-House	OP	9.00	14.00
1996-03-13750	1st Communion Girl	In-House	OP	9.00	14.00
1996-03-13751	Sailor Girl	In-House	OP	10.00	15.00
1996-03-13752	School Girl	In-House	OP	9.00	14.00
1996-03-13753	School Boy	In-House	OP	9.00	14.00
1996-03-13754	Country Girl Plaid	In-House	OP	9.00	14.00
1996-03-13755	Fisherman	In-House	OP	10.00	15.00
1996-03-13756	Winter Boy	In-House	OP	10.00	15.00
1996-03-13757	School Girl	In-House	OP	9.00	14.00
1996-03-13758	Country Girl	In-House	OP	9.00	14.00
1996-03-13759	Country Boy	In-House	OP	9.00	14.00
1996-03-13760	Sheriff	In-House	OP	10.00	15.00
1996-03-13761	Prep School Girl	In-House	OP	10.00	15.00
1996-03-13780	Santa Bear	In-House	OP	9.00	14.00
1996-03-13765-1	Napoleon	In-House	OP	9.00	12.00
1996-03-13765-2	Musketeer	In-House	OP	9.00	12.00
1996-03-13765-3	Princess	In-House	OP	9.00	12.00
1996-03-13765-4	Lady-In-Waiting	In-House	OP	9.00	12.00
1996-03-13761	Prep School Girl	In-House	OP	10.00	15.00
1996-03-13739	Sherlock	In-House	OP	10.00	15.00
1996-03-13762	Royal Guard	In-House	OP	10.00	15.00
1996-03-13763	Robin	In-House	OP	10.00	15.00
1996-03-13764	Genie	In-House	OP	9.00	14.00
1996-03-13767	Peter	In-House	OP	9.00	14.00
1996-03-13768	Little Bo Peep	In-House	OP	10.00	15.00
1996-03-13715	Jester	In-House	OP	9.00	14.00
1996-03-13716	Le Artiste	In-House	OP	9.00	14.00

RUSS® BERRIE AND COMPANY – TEDDYTOWN™ VILLAGE COLLECTION

RELEASE YEAR	FIGURINE	ARTIST	EDITION	ISSUE	QUOTE
1995-01-13902	Flower Shop	In-House	OP	7.50	7.50
1995-01-13903	Hospital	In-House	OP	7.50	7.50
1995-01-13904	Fruit Store	In-House	OP	7.50	7.50
1995-01-13905	Honey Restaurant	In-House	OP	7.50	7.50
1995-01-13906	Teddy Bakery	In-House	OP	7.50	7.50
1995-01-13907	School	In-House	OP	7.50	7.50
1995-01-13924	Wishing Well	In-House	OP	8.00	8.00
1995-01-13925	The Artist	In-House	OP	5.00	5.00
1995-01-13926	Family Dinner	In-House	OP	7.00	7.00
1995-01-13927	Fruit Stand	In-House	OP	7.00	7.00
1995-01-13928	The Baseball Game	In-House	OP	5.00	5.00
1995-01-13929	In The Garden	In-House	OP	5.00	5.00
1995-01-13834	Boo Boo Bear	In-House	OP	2.50	2.50
1995-01-13835	Milk Truck	In-House	OP	6.00	6.00
1995-01-13836	School Bus	In-House	OP	6.00	6.00
1995-01-13837	Nurse	In-House	OP	6.00	6.00
1995-01-13838	Doctor	In-House	OP	6.00	6.00

SARAH'S ATTIC® – MICHAUD COLLECTION

RELEASE YEAR	FIGURINE	ARTIST	EDITION	ISSUE	QUOTE
1992-03-070	Professor Bear 3906	Michaud	RT12/95	24.00	29.00
1992-03-071	Tommy's Bear 3907	Michaud	RT12/95	24.00	29.00
1992-03-072	Irish Bear 3908	Michaud	RT12/95	24.00	29.00
1992-03-073	Just Ted Bear 3909	Michaud	RT12/95	24.00	29.00
1992-03-074	Dowager Twins Bear 3910	Michaud	RT12/95	24.00	29.00
1992-03-075	Me And My Shadow Bear 3911	Michaud	RT12/95	24.00	29.00
1992-03-076	Second Hand-Rose Bear 3912	Michaud	RT12/95	24.00	29.00
1992-03-077	Witchie Bear 3913	Michaud	RT1994	24.00	29.00
1992-03-078	Bellhop Bear 3914	Michaud	RT1995	24.00	29.00
1992-03-079	Eddie Bear 3915	Michaud	RT1994	24.00	29.00
1992-03-080	Librarian Bear 3916	Michaud	RT1994	24.00	29.00
1992-03-081	Aunt Eunice Bear 3917	Michaud	RT1995	24.00	24.00
1992-03-082	Eddie W/Trunk 3918	Michaud	RT1995	40.00	40.00
1992-03-083	Librarian W/Desk 3919	Michaud	RT1995	40.00	50.00
1992-03-084	Bellhop & Second-Hand Rose 3920	Michaud	RT1995	40.00	50.00
1992-03-085	Witchie W/Pot 3921	Michaud	RT1994	40.00	50.00
1992-03-086	Tommy W/Dog 3922	Michaud	RT1995	40.00	50.00
1992-03-087	Just Ted W/Mirror 3923	Michaud	RT1995	40.00	50.00
1992-03-088	Aunt Eunice Bathtime 3924	Michaud	RT1995	40.00	50.00
1992-03-089	Professor W/Board 3925	Michaud	RT1995	40.00	50.00
1992-03-090	Me and My Shadow W/Chair 3926	Michaud	RT1994	45.00	45.00
1992-03-091	Dowager Twins On Couch 3927	Michaud	RT1994	60.00	70.00
1992-03-092	Irish Bear At Pub 3928	Michaud	OP1995	40.00	50.00
1992-03-093	Michaud Bear Sign 3929	Michaud	RT1995	35.00	45.00
1995-03-097	Proxy Bear 4332	Michaud/Sarah's Attic	RT12/95	20.00	20.00
1995-03-098	Proxy W/Jewelry Box 4333	Michaud/Sarah's Attic	RT12/95	33.00	33.00
1995-03-099	Bay City Beauty 4334	Michaud/Sarah's Attic	RT12/95	26.00	26.00
1995-03-100	Bay City Beauty W/Trunk 4335	Michaud/Sarah's Attic	RT12/95	40.00	40.00
1995-03-101	Love Heals All 4438	Michaud/Sarah's Attic	OP	28.00	28.00

SCHMID – ROOSEVELT BEARS™

RELEASE YEAR	FIGURINE	ARTIST	EDITION	ISSUE	QUOTE
1993-01-9000	Roosevelt Bears In Traveling Suits	A. Gustafson	RT 1995	25.00	30.00
1993-01-9001	Roosevelt Bears As Patriots	A. Gustafson	RT 1995	25.00	30.00
1993-01-9002	Roosevelt Bears In Swim Suits	A. Gustafson	RT 1995	25.00	30.00
1993-01-9003	Roosevelt Bears In Clown Suits	A. Gustafson	RT 1995	25.00	30.00
1993-01-9004	Roosevelt Bears In Military Uniforms	A. Gustafson	RT 1995	25.00	30.00
1993-01-9005	Roosevelt Bears in Baseball Suits	A. Gustafson	RT 1995	25.00	30.00
1994-01-96822	Roosevelt Bears Fight Fires	A. Gustafson	RT 1995	25.00	30.00
1994-01-96823	Roosevelt Bears Do The Cake Walk Dance	A. Gustafson	RT 1995	25.00	30.00
1994-01-96824	Roosevelt Bears As Organ Grinders	A. Gustafson	RT 1995	25.00	30.00
1994-01-96825	Roosevelt Bears Go Fishing	A. Gustafson	RT 1995	25.00	30.00
1994-01-96826	Roosevelt Bears As Indians	A. Gustafson	RT 1995	25.00	30.00
1994-01-96926	Roosevelt Bears Graduates	A. Gustafson	RT 1995	25.00	30.00

STEIFF USA, L.P. – PETER FAGAN

RELEASE YEAR	FIGURINE	ARTIST	EDITION	ISSUE	QUOTE
1994-01-612657	Baerle (1904) and Roly Poly (1909)	P. Fagan	OP	20.00	20.00
1994-01-612671	Teddy Rose (1925)	P. Fagan	OP	20.00	20.00
1995-01-612701	Zotty (1951) and Tiger (1955)	P. Fagan	OP	20.00	20.00

UNITED DESIGN® CORP. – TEDDY ANGELS™

RELEASE YEAR	FIGURINE	ARTIST	EDITION	ISSUE	QUOTE
1995-01-001	Sweetie	P. J. Jonas	OP	7.50	7.50
1995-01-002	Cowboy	P.J. Jonas	OP	9.50	9.50
1995-01-003	Ivy and Blankie	P. J. Jonas	OP	6.50	6.50
1995-01-004	Murray and Little Bit	P. J. Jonas	OP	9.50	9.50
1995-01-005	Murray Mending Bruin	P. J. Jonas	OP	7.50	7.50
1995-01-006	Old Bear and Little Bit Reading	P. J. Jonas	OP	7.50	7.50
1995-01-007	Bunny's Picnic	P. J. Jonas	OP	9.50	9.50
1995-01-008	Casey Tucking Honey In	P. J. Jonas	OP	9.50	9.50
1995-01-009	Ivy In Garden	P. J. Jonas	OP	7.50	7.50
1995-01-010	Tilli and Murray	P. J. Jonas	OP	7.50	7.50
1995-01-011	Old Bear	P. J. Jonas	OP	9.50	9.50
1995-01-012	Bruin Making Valentines	P. J. Jonas	OP	7.50	7.50
1995-01-013	Bruin and Blue Birds	P. J. Jonas	OP	9.50	9.50
1995-01-014	Honey	P. J. Jonas	OP	6.50	6.50
1995-01-015	Tilli and Doves	P. J. Jonas	OP	9.50	9.50
1995-01-016	Sweetie and Santa Bear	P. J. Jonas	OP	11.00	11.00

United Design® Corp. – TEDDY ANGELS™

Release Year	Figurine	Artist	Edition	Issue	Quote
1995-01-017	Casey	P. J. Jonas	OP	6.50	6.50
1995-01-018	Ivy	P. J. Jonas	OP	6.50	6.50
1995-01-021	Bruin With Harp Seal Pup	P. J. Jonas	OP	UD	UD
1995-01-022	Murray With Angel	P. J. Jonas	OP	UD	UD
1995-01-023	Casey and Honey Reading	P. J. Jonas	OP	UD	UD
1995-01-024	Nicholas With Net Of Stars	P. J. Jonas	OP	UD	UD
1995-01-025	Sweetie With Kitty Cats	P. J. Jonas	OP	UD	UD
1995-01-026	Old Bear and Little Bit Gardening	P. J. Jonas	OP	UD	UD
1995-01-027	Rufus Helps A Bird	P. J. Jonas	OP	UD	UD
1995-01-028	Ivy With Locket	P. J. Jonas	OP	UD	UD

Vicki Lane Creative Design – NIGHT BEAR-FORE CHRISTMAS

Release Year	Figurine	Artist	Edition	Issue	Quote
1987-01-1252	Christmas Tree With Teddy	V. Anderson	OP	21.00	21.00
1990-01-1144	Little Sister	V. Anderson	OP	14.00	14.00
1992-01-1161	Mother and Bear Child	V. Anderson	OP	30.00	30.00
1992-01-10051	Black Iron Stove	V. Anderson	OP	16.00	16.00
1993-01-10072	Fire Place	V. Anderson	OP	20.00	20.00
1993-01-1255	Papa Bear With Presents	V. Anderson	OP	22.00	22.00
1993-01-1256	Sparky	V. Anderson	OP	21.00	21.00
1993-01-1257	Sugar Plum	V. Anderson	OP	22.00	22.00
1993-01-1258	Roseberry Sleeping By The Clock	V. Anderson	OP	22.00	22.00
1993-01-1259	"It's Bedtime Fuzzy"	V. Anderson	OP	22.50	22.50
1993-01-1260	Grandpa And Grandma	V. Anderson	OP	25.00	25.00
1993-01-1261	Snowman With Bears	V. Anderson	OP	24.00	24.00

Notes